Heart & Soul Connection

Heart & Soul Connection:

A Devotional Guide to Marriage, Service & Love

Grihastha Vision Team

The Grihastha Vision Team (GVT) was born of necessity. The members are counselors and educators who bring a wealth of spiritual and material experience to this project. The biographical information at the end of each chapter will reveal the diversity of the group and the broad range of services in which they have been engaged.

When the GVT founders came together in 2003, they were committed to put into practice a variety of initiatives designed to contribute to the healthy development of all devotees, especially couples, children, and families. The synergy that comes from a common objective in service to Krishna and His devotees has resulted in a group that works harmoniously and collaboratively in its many endeavors. Initiatives that have been accomplished to date are as follows:

Development of a four-day intensive marriage and family course, entitled Strengthening the Bonds That Free Us, which has been taught around the world

Establishment of marriage mentor trainings and programs

Publication of educational pamphlets and a Directory of Vaishnava Marriage Educators, Counselors, and Matrimonial Services

Development of a resource-rich website: www.VaisnavaFamilyResources.org

Establishment of a pledge of support whereby ISKCON leaders and managers commit to support the grihastha ashrama

Free public teleconferences on marriage and family topics

Ongoing provision of workshops on a variety of marriage-related topics throughout ISKCON worldwide

Design & Typography by Relish New Brand Experience

ISBN-13: 978-1530642717

Dedication & Acknowledgements

THIS BOOK IS DEDICATED to His Divine Grace A. C. Bhaktivedanta Swami Srila Prabhupada, the beloved Founder-*Acharya* of the International Society for Krishna Consciousness.

May His Divine Grace empower us with his unparalleled ability to touch the hearts and souls of others with compassion and understanding.

Special acknowledgements:

To Anuttama dasa, Grihastha Vision Team (GVT) member who suggested the perfect title – *Heart & Soul Connection: A Devotional Guide to Marriage, Service & Love.*

To all the other dedicated, visionary GVT members: Arcana Siddhi devi dasi, Cintamani devi dasi, Jagannatha Pandit dasa, Karnamrita dasa, Mantrini devi dasi, Partha dasa, Praharana devi dasi, Sridevi dasi, Tamohara dasa, Tariq Saleem Ziyad, and Uttama devi dasi, who put untold and unpaid hours into writing this book and into creating and implementing many other marriage and family strengthening initiatives for the benefit of children, couples and families everywhere.

To Partha dasa for his creative and funny potato cartoons.

To Chelsea Blackerby and Mike Wohlwend, founders of Pixelsit web design studio, who began the concept for our book cover, and to Yamuna Jivana dasa of Blugod Tattoos and Piercings, who designed the final cover.

To the reviewers who took their precious time to scrutinize this book and give their valuable feedback.

To the kind and generous devotees who assisted in the publication of this book including:

Praharana devi dasi, Todd & Amanda Wahlstrom (Guru dasa & Rati Manjari devi dasi), Kunti devi dasi & Madhavacharya dasa, Akrura dasa (Gita Coaching), and Srinivas & Sangeetha Bhat.

A big hug and immeasurable gratitude to Vrnda devi who edited this book with so much professionalism, dedication, time, and love – she took our rough draft and shaped it into a powerful, practical, beautiful book.

And to the readers who pick up this book, we pray to Lord Sri Chaitanya that it will penetrate your hearts and empower you with healthy, strong, devotional relationships and families.

Krsnanandini devi dasi
President, Grihastha Vision Team

Contents

Foreword: The Purpose of the Grihastha Ashrama

His Holiness Giriraj Swami

WHEN I FIRST JOINED the Boston temple in 1969, we all were quite young, and not many of us were married. And we were so new to Krishna consciousness and so dependent on Srila Prabhupada that we asked him for guidance in every area. One of the lady devotees, Balai devi dasi, had recently gotten married and wasn't sure what her relationship with her husband should be. She asked Srila Prabhupada, and he replied, "Just as the right hand has a relationship with the left hand through the body, so you have a relationship with your husband through Krishna, with Krishna in the center." There is the right hand, and there is the left hand; but what connects them is the body. In this example, the right and left hands are the husband and wife, and the body is Krishna.

We had to change our consciousness, Srila Prabhupada told us, and put Krishna at the center. That, he said, would make all the difference. When our false ego is at the center, we have so many problems, but when Krishna is at the center, our relationships become harmonious.

We come into the material world out of envy of Krishna. We want to take the position of Krishna and be the enjoyer, the controller, the proprietor. This is our mood in conditioned existence. And when we come into the material world, we end up competing not only with Krishna, but also with so many other competitors of Krishna. And that egoistic mood can enter the home. We compete to be the enjoyers, the controllers, and the proprietors, and that leads to conflict – so many imitation gods fighting for supremacy. Through the process of Krishna consciousness, our false, bodily identification is replaced by the realization of our true identity as *gopi-bhartuh pada-kamalayor dasa-dasanudasah* – the servant of the servant of the servant of the servant of Krishna, the maintainer of the *gopis*.

When a disciple asked Srila Prabhupada, "What should we do when there are conflicts among the devotees?" he replied, "If each devotee thinks, 'I am the servant of the servant of the servant of Krishna,' then there will be no more conflict." The same principle applies in the home. If each family member thinks and feels, "I am the servant of the servant of the servant of Krishna," the relationships will be very congenial. But that requires a revolution in consciousness. We are in the material world because we want to be the master of the master of the masters, and that mentality leads to frustration, disappointment, and death – repeated birth and death. Becoming the servant of the servant of the servants of Krishna leads to happiness and ultimate liberation.

Soon after I first met Srila Prabhupada and the devotees, I heard that Srila Prabhupada's spiritual master, Srila Bhaktisiddhanta Sarasvati Thakura, had said that when you come to Krishna consciousness, you become relieved of the burden of enjoyment. As a university student in Boston, I was actually feeling that burden, because every weekend there would be a very strong competition for who would enjoy the most. Leading up to the weekend, the students – and perhaps the faculty too – were making plans how to enjoy. These plans included going to restaurants, going to movies, going to shows, going to parties, going to clubs – so many plans. I didn't really like any of those activities, and it was a burden for me to have to enjoy like the others. And then the students would ask each other, "What did you do? Where did you go?"... "Oh, I went to a party. We all got high and..."... "Oh, I went out on a date and..."

The statement that when you become a devotee you become relieved of the burden of enjoying resonated with me. It was artificial for me to try to enjoy like that. It was artificial because as souls our real pleasure comes in relationship with the Supreme Soul. True love exists only in relation to Krishna. The *Bhakti-rasamrta-sindhu*[1] defines pure love, *prema*, as the focusing of all one's loving propensities and feelings on the Supreme Lord.

> *ananya-mamata visnau*
> *mamata prema-sangata*
> *bhaktir ity ucyate bhisma-*
> *prahladoddhava-naradaih*

When one develops an unflinching sense of ownership or possessiveness in relation to Lord Vishnu, or, in other words, when one thinks Vishnu and no one else to be the only object of love, such an awakening is called bhakti [devotion] by exalted persons like Bhishma, Prahlada, Uddhava, and Narada.

> [*Bhakti-rasamrta-sindhu* 1.4.2, as quoted
> in *Chaitanya-charitamrita, Madhya* 23.8]

Queen Kunti prayed some beautiful prayers to her nephew Lord Krishna:

atha visvesa visvatman
visva-murte svakesu me
sneha-pasam imam chindhi
drdham pandusu vrsnisu

O Lord of the universe, soul of the universe, O personality of the form of the universe, please, therefore, sever my tie of affection for my kinsmen, the Pandavas and the Vrishnis.

[*Srimad-Bhagavatam* 1.8.41]

tvayi me 'nanya-visaya
matir madhu-pate 'sakrt
ratim udvahatad addha
gangevaugham udanvati

O Lord of Madhu, as the Ganges forever flows to the sea without hindrance, let my attraction be constantly drawn unto You without being diverted to anyone else.

[*Srimad-Bhagavatam* 1.8.42]

As we become serious in Krishna consciousness, this really becomes our prayer, "Let my love flow to Krishna without any hindrance, just as the Ganges flows to the ocean." These statements, "Please sever my attachments for my family members. Let my love flow exclusively unto You without being diverted to anyone else," raise some questions. What about other relationships? What happens to my relationships with my friends and family?

In his purport, Srila Prabhupada makes a very interesting point. He says that Kunti's family members were devotees of Krishna. Her paternal family members, the Vrishnis, were devotees, and her sons, the Pandavas, were devotees. And affection for devotees is not outside the pale of Krishna consciousness, of pure devotional service. So when Kunti prays, "Please sever my ties of affection for my kinsmen," she means that she wants the affection based on the body to be cut.

> Her affection for the Pandavas and the Vrishnis is not out of the range of devotional service because the service of the Lord and the service of the devotees are identical. Sometimes service to the devotee is more valuable than service to the Lord. But here the affection of Kunti devi for the Pandavas and the Vrishnis was due to family relation. This tie of affection in terms of material relations is the relation of maya [illusion] because the relations of the body or the mind are due to the influence of the external energy. Relations of the soul, established in relation with

the Supreme Soul, are factual relations. When Kunti devi wanted to cut off the family relation, she meant to cut off the relation of the skin. The skin relation is the cause of material bondage, but the relation of the soul is the cause of freedom. This relation of the soul to the soul can be established by the medium of the relation with the Supersoul.

[*Srimad-Bhagavatam* 1.8.42, purport]

There are two categories of affection – one based on the body and one based on the soul, soul-to-soul, through the medium of the Supersoul, the Supreme Soul. When Kunti prays, "Please sever my ties of affection for my kinsmen," she means the affection that is based on the body – so that only the affection based on the soul remains. Affection based on the body leads to bondage and death, whereas affection based on the soul leads to liberation and eternal life.

So, we don't have to give up our family relationships, but we want to purify them. We want the material aspect, which is based on the body, to become less and less prominent, and we want the spiritual aspect, which is based on the soul through the medium of the Supreme Soul, to become more and more prominent. The more the spiritual dimension of our relationships becomes prominent, the more our relationships become congenial to our happiness and ultimate success in life.

One authority on marriage said, "Marriage is not supposed to make you happy. It's supposed to make you married; and once you are safely and totally married, you have a structure of security and support from which you can find your own happiness."[2] We are not in any illusion that marriage per se will bring us happiness, but we want to work on our marriages so that we can function well as parts of a unit, the family unit, and within the relative peace and mutual support of that unit find our own inner happiness, which is the only real happiness there is.

The marital relationship also provides the basis for the couple's children to develop Krishna consciousness and be happy. Sometime later, Srila Prabhupada wrote to Balai dasi:

> In materialistic marriages generally there are too many troubles and frustrations because the basic principle for both the husband and wife is their own personal sense gratification. Therefore there is inevitable conflict and divorce petition. But in a Krishna Conscious marriage the basic principle is for both husband and wife to serve Krishna nicely and to help the partner advance in spiritual life. In this way both the husband and wife are true benefactors for one another and there is no question of any serious conflicts or separation. So I am sure that to have such nice parents who are devotees of Lord Krishna, your child Nandini is very, very fortunate. In *Bhagavad-gita* Krishna instructs us that for one to be born in the family of devotees means that such

person was the most pious of all living entities. So raise Nandini very carefully in Krishna Consciousness, and surely Krishna will bestow all blessings upon you and your family.

[Letter to Balai, 21 July 1969]

We often hear at *japa* retreats, "I wish I had heard these things about *japa* thirty years ago," but better late than never. Some older couples may be thinking, "I wish I had heard these things about grihastha ashrama thirty years ago," but better late than never. And some of the younger ones may think, "I am so glad I read this book so early in my marriage, for I am being guided from the very beginning about what possibilities to expect and how to deal with them." But for those who are older, the soul is eternal, and Krishna consciousness is eternal, and our relationships based on Krishna consciousness are also eternal. So even if in a relative, material sense we are starting late, it is never too late, and in relation to eternal time we are just developing the proper mood of loving service that will continue into eternity.

These material bodies are just dresses for the soul. Our identities based on the body and mind are temporary and illusory. Our real identities are as loving servants of Krishna and His devotees, and whatever we are doing here in the material world is practice for our eternal life in the spiritual world where we will serve Krishna and His devotees in ecstatic love. As Srila Prabhupada said, if a high school student is doing college-level work, he can be promoted to college. So, if we are in the material world but are engaged in the activities of the spiritual world, we can be promoted to the spiritual world. The basic activity of the spiritual world, which includes chanting the holy names and glories of Sri Krishna, is to render loving service to Krishna and the other servants of Krishna. And the grihastha ashrama is a suitable situation for practicing loving service, which can qualify us for eternal loving service in the spiritual world. Hare Krishna.

HIS HOLINESS GIRIRAJ SWAMI has toured extensively throughout India and many other countries, carrying knowledge of Krishna and helping to develop Srila Prabhupada's mission. He is a sannyasi, an initiating guru in ISKCON, and a member of the Governing Body Commission (GBC). He has taught at the Vaishnava Institute for Higher Education in Vrindavana, India, and now gives presentations at *japa* retreats and workshops for the Bhagavat Life educational foundation. Although health considerations have recently limited his traveling, Giriraj Swami has taken this as an opportunity to focus on one of Srila Prabhupada's personal instructions: to write. Now based in Southern California, he is the author of *Watering the Seed* (Mountain King Books, 2000) and is a frequent contributor to *Back to Godhead* magazine. He is working on several publications, including books about his search for a spiritual master and his early days in the Boston temple, his travels with Srila Prabhupada in India from 1970 to 1972, and Srila Prabhupada's monumental efforts in Bombay.

Introduction

Cintamani devi dasi &
Jagannatha Pandit dasa

THE BOOK YOU ARE HOLDING in your hands, *Heart & Soul Connection: A Devotional Guide to Marriage, Service & Love*, is a heartfelt offering written to assist devotees on their paths to obtain the deepest desires of their hearts: to love Krishna, to serve one another, and to share spirituality by word and deed.

Loving Krishna with our hearts and souls is one of the deepest desires of the Vaishnavas...

> Although one may develop innumerable saintly qualities, without love of Krishna one will not achieve complete success. One must understand the Personality of Godhead as He is and love Him. Even if one is not capable of analytically understanding the position of God, if one simply loves Krishna, then one is certainly perfect. Many of the residents of Vrindavana had no idea that Krishna is the Supreme Personality of Godhead, nor did they know of Krishna's potencies or incarnations. They simply loved Krishna with their hearts and souls, and therefore they are considered most perfect.
>
> [*Srimad-Bhagavatam* 11.11.33, purport]

Pleasing the Vaishnavas is another of the deepest desires of the Vaishnavas...

> [Haridasa Thakura] always accepted the good qualities of Vaishnavas and never found fault in them. He engaged his heart and soul only to satisfy the Vaishnavas.
>
> [*Chaitanya-charitamrita*, Adi 8.62]

Sharing the message of Lord Chaitanya with tolerance and humility is also one of the deepest desires of the Vaishnavas...

At least the followers of Chaitanya Mahaprabhu must come out of India to preach His cult all over the world, for this is the mission of Lord Chaitanya. The followers of Lord Chaitanya must execute His will with heart and soul, being more tolerant than the trees and humbler than the straw in the street.

[*Chaitanya-charitamrita, Adi* 9.47, purport]

How can a book about marriage assist us in obtaining the ultimate goal of life? We could start by speaking about its important and relevant content, the years in preparation before its publication, or the experience and expertise of the contributors. While all these are essential in answering that question, we would first like you to consider that *this* book about marriage is more than just a book. It *appears* that it is simply an object of a particular size and shape, made of paper with pages on which there is ink shaped in the form of words – words that may be educational, interesting, or inspiring. However, beyond the *words*, what you are holding in your hands is a physical manifestation of – simply put – love.

Why do we say love? Because the existence of each word on each page is due to the dedication, determination, and sacrifice of a group of devotees with whom we are honored to have association – the North American Grihastha Vision Team (GVT). This book exists because this grass-roots team of mature devotees has dedicated their lives to ensure that the grihastha ashrama, the shelter provided by spiritual family life, develops and expands as the productive component of society that Srila Prabhupada, Founder-*Acharya* of the International Society for Krishna Consciousness (ISKCON), intended it to be. This team of devotees is determined that devotees entering marriage are properly prepared, that those already married are fortified with additional knowledge and skills, and that ISKCON's leaders and members serve as educated supporters. This team of devotees is committed to offering time, energy, and resources to make these goals a reality.

The dedication of this team was such that each word was given careful consideration. Each topic and concept was carefully weighed in terms of how it may or may not benefit the devotees. Great thought was given on how to ensure that the presentation was clear, that the information was relevant and meaningful, and that it would meet the needs of a broad range of devotees. Consideration was also given on how to be respectful of devotees' sensibilities – as some topics might be considered sensitive. Devotees of varied ages, ashramas, and stages of life reviewed this book before publication to ensure that it would be a useful and inspiring offering. The goal of these efforts was to make sure that this book would prove to be an important gift to our society. When an offering is made from the heart with love as its guiding force, then the offering is empowered.

The book you are about to read has the power to transform your perception and experience of household life in Krishna consciousness. This transformative power is due to the love and dedication that went into it. Receive it in that spirit. In this way, even if there is something that does not resonate with you, stay open to the spirit of the work. It can create opportunities for greater dialogue and exchange that can contribute even more to the growth of the grihastha ashrama and Srila Prabhupada's mission.

The content of the book gives scripturally-based and practical strategies to help devotees use the grihastha ashrama for its highest purpose: going home, back to Godhead. The broad range of topics is critical for successfully negotiating the challenges that come with household life and for deeply appreciating the blessings and joys that come with it as well.

The opening chapter presents the foundational principles that support Krishna conscious family life based on Srila Prabhupada's teachings. These principles and values are woven throughout the subsequent chapters. Understanding such topics as the roles of husband and wife, social responsibility, affection and intimacy, and finances, to name a few, are necessary for devotee marriages to flourish.

A book of this nature is surely long overdue and hopefully will inspire other similar works. *Heart & Soul Connection: A Devotional Guide to Marriage, Service & Love* significantly highlights the growth-enhancing potential of the grihastha ashrama.

The intention of the GVT's endeavors, including this book, is to make a valuable contribution to Srila Prabhupada's mission. As His Holiness Bhakti Tirtha Maharaja, a strong supporter of women, children, and families, stated:

> When we start seeing more and more families being able to stay together and honor their spiritual lives while taking care of their material lives, then we will know that we (as an institution) are on the rise... being able to make our household ashrama more spiritual, covering spiritual and material needs, is actually one of the greatest offerings that we can make to Srila Prabhupada. It will be the greatest sign that our movement works and the greatest sign that we can offer people a positive alternative.
>
> [Lecture at Gita-Nagari, 31 October 1999]

As you embark on your exploration of *Heart & Soul Connection*, we pray that the contents are useful and inspiring – for yourself and for your service to others. As we deepen our relationships with ourselves and others – essentially, with Krishna – we are moving forward to fulfill the deepest desire of our hearts and souls: pure love of God.

About the Authors

GVT

CINTAMANI DEVI DASI (Courtney B Parks, PhD), initiated by His Holiness Bhakti Tirtha Maharaja in 1992, is a resident of Gita-Nagari Dhama, a farm and temple community in Pennsylvania, where she seeks to serve and support the devotees, manage His Holiness Bhakti Tirtha Maharaja's projects, and care for her family. Her profession is psychotherapy, and she currently serves as a clinical supervisor for a large social service agency. In this capacity, she mentors family therapists and provides trainings for the agency, including a 12-hour parenting class for foster parents and staff. She and her husband, Jagannatha Pandit dasa, provide counseling for devotees and workshops on topics such as relationships, grief and loss, and parenting. They have been married since 1991 and have two daughters.

JAGANNATHA PANDIT DASA (James E Parks), initiated by His Holiness Bhakti Tirtha Maharaja in 1992, is engaged in a number of services at Gita-Nagari Dhama. He has served as a member of the Gita-Nagari management board and currently is a member of the Gita-Nagari brahminical council. He also serves as a *pujari* for Sri Sri Radha Damodara, the principal Deities of Gita-Nagari, and assists with various projects on the farm. Professionally, he is a counselor at a youth facility where he provides individual and group counseling to adolescent boys. He designs curricula and facilitates psycho-educational groups for youth on a broad variety of topics such as stress management, employment skills, and values clarification. He also designs and provides cultural diversity trainings for staff. Both Cintamani devi dasi and Jagannatha Pandit dasa are members of the North American Grihastha Vision Team.

Chapter 1 Foundations: Twelve Principles for Successful Krishna Conscious Family Life

Praharana devi dasi

In this chapter you will learn:

✓ Twelve Principles Compiled from Srila Prabhupada's Teachings

✓ How Principles and Values Serve as a Framework for Spiritual Life

✓ The Role of Principles and Values in Krishna Conscious Family Life

✓ What Srila Prabhupada said about Krishna Conscious Family Life

Innocent potato comes to fork in the road of life

Principles and Values as a Framework for Spiritual Life

Beginning of Spiritual Life – Spiritual life is not automatic. When we take up God consciousness, there is a profound shift in the way we live our lives. These changes, although blissful and exciting, involve practice and discipline. As part of our spiritual evolution, we accept and practice moral principles such as strict vegetarianism, fidelity in marriage, and avoidance of gambling and intoxication. We also adopt spiritual practices such as mantra meditation, scripture study, and service to our temple and devotional community. All of these changes are based on the acceptance of Krishna conscious principles and values as taught to us by His Divine Grace A. C. Bhaktivedanta Swami Prabhupada, Founder-*Acharya* of the International Society for Krishna Consciousness. Understanding principles and values is important; when challenges or problems arise in life, principles and values serve as a spiritual context for finding solutions and give us a framework for growth.

Living Spiritual Principles is the Challenge – Principles in spiritual life become guiding ideals for how to live a spiritual life. The challenge is not simply to accept a principle – the challenge is to *act* on it. Acceptance can seem uncomplicated, but living by principles and values is often not so easy. Our practical actions are an actual mirror of our consciousness and a public expression of our faith and commitment. As we evolve and advance in spiritual life, adherence to spiritual principles and values transforms our behavior – our social and personal relationships.

Principles and Values in Krishna Conscious Family Life

Purpose of the Grihastha Ashrama – In married life, we not only live in a spiritual ashrama where there is the opportunity to make great spiritual advancement, but we also take responsibility for supporting other ashramas and implementing social change. And, as Srila Prabhupada said in Tehran in 1976, "If there [are] no householders, then wherefrom the saintly persons will come? They will not drop from the sky."

It is a big undertaking. However, this ashrama also affords stability and happiness. The grihastha ashrama is the prescribed method of spiritual advancement for almost every devotee and lasts throughout most of our adult lives.

Introduction to the Twelve Principles – In grihastha life, we can create a joyful, peaceful, and spiritual environment for the whole family and the whole community. This requires living our lives consciously – driven by application of certain Krishna conscious principles and values for family life. The North America Grihastha Vision Team has compiled twelve main categories of principles based on the teachings of Srila Prabhupada. You will find, in studying and applying the various chapters in this book, that these Twelve Principles for Successful Krishna Conscious Family Life are referred to time and again. The idea is that by applying them in many contexts, they will become truly integrated into our daily lives. Each principle is explored through

Twelve Principles
for
Successful Krishna Conscious Family Life

1

Alignment with Srila Prabhupada

2

Spiritual Growth and Progress

3

Spiritual Equality / Material Difference

4

Positive and Realistic Vision

5

Mutual Respect and Appreciation

6

Commitment and Dedication

7

Open and Honest Communication

8

Personal and Social Responsibility

9

Economic Development and Prosperity

10

Focus on Children's Welfare

11

Family Love and Affection

12

Regulated, Balanced, and Exemplary Lifestyle

quotes and examples from Srila Prabhupada and from scripture. Each chapter in this book will refer to these principles and values as central to the learning and to the practical experience.

Lord Krishna in the Center – The Twelve Principles for Successful Krishna Conscious Family Life effectively put Krishna in the center of grihastha life. They become the basis for life, action, and growth. They provide not only a guiding ideal, but a foundation for practical action and experience. Embracing them with joy and spiritual enthusiasm will not only result in happy and healthy family life, but will also serve as a practical social example.

Twelve Principles Compiled from Srila Prabhupada's Teachings

PRINCIPLE #1 – Alignment with Srila Prabhupada

Following the Teachings and Example of Srila Prabhupada – Spiritual life in Krishna consciousness is integrally aligned with the teachings and example of Srila Prabhupada. He gave us instructions on how to live a spiritually sound family life consistent with Vaishnava traditions and practices. The Twelve Principles for Successful Krishna Conscious Family Life represent those teachings. Because Krishna consciousness has become a world-wide movement, there are cultural variations in the practical application of Srila Prabhupada's teachings. This is consistent with the instruction to adjust for time, place and circumstance.

Unity in Diversity – Understanding the Twelve Principles for Successful Krishna Conscious Family Life assists the devotees in transposing Srila Prabhupada's teachings to apply them in a particular cultural environment. For example, in some cultures the roles of husband and wife are very traditional and conservative. In other societies this might not be the norm. It may not be recommended or practical for a devotee couple living in a Western country to rigorously follow a strictly Vedic model of family life. Srila Prabhupada broke with Vedic traditional roles for women by equally encouraging women in the West to live in the Temple ashrama and to take part in outreach, deity worship, and many other activities. From this we understand that he adapted Krishna consciousness to Western values of gender equality, thereby endorsing diversity, while maintaining the unity of the universal truths of Krishna consciousness. In other words, in ISKCON we are united in our practice of Krishna consciousness, but we are also diverse in our languages, cultures, normative gender roles, and ethnic backgrounds. Srila Prabhupada encouraged his disciples to use their intelligence to apply spiritual principles in diverse situations as a means to live together peacefully.

What did Srila Prabhupada teach us about abiding by the order of the spiritual master?

> Srila Vishvanatha Cakravarti Thakura states that one should not care very much whether he is going to be liberated or not, but he should simply execute the direct order received from the spiritual master. If one sticks to the principle of abiding by the order of the spiritual master, he will always remain in a liberated position.
>
> [*Srimad-Bhagavatam* 4.20.13, purport]

PRINCIPLE #2 – Spiritual Growth and Progress

Grihastha Ashrama: A Place of Personal Growth – Srila Prabhupada taught that family life and the home itself should be an ashrama, a place for spiritual culture and practice. Grihastha life affords the opportunity for personal growth in many ways – spiritual, emotional, economical, and social. Successful family life involves supporting the other ashramas that are, by their nature, financially dependent. It is an ashrama of responsibility, charity, and maturity. Of course, mutual respect and support between all the ashramas is essential for a healthy society.

Gradual Process of Renunciation in Grihastha Life – Vaishnava theology and practice extols renunciation and sacrifice at all stages of life. For most devotees, becoming truly renounced is a gradual process. As a devotee becomes more mature in spiritual life, an internal transformation takes place over time, and renunciation becomes natural and blissful. Trying to force oneself or others to artificially renounce before spiritual maturity is attained will not lead to true spiritual advancement; instead, one runs the risk of falling down. Srila Prabhupada has given us a perfect process. We can trust his wisdom and guidance.

What did Srila Prabhupada teach us about making advancement in household life?

> Anyone who takes to Krishna consciousness, he is first class, that's all. So our principle should be how to make people Krishna conscious, God conscious. Then our mission will be successful. Either as gri-hastha, as a vanaprastha, as sannyasi, it doesn't matter. Philosophy, the truth, should be preached. Everyone will be happy. That is Krishna consciousness.
>
> [Lecture on *Srimad-Bhagavatam* 3.22.20, Tehran, 9 August 1976]

> It is not that only sannyasis, vanaprasthas and brahmacharis can reach Krishna. A grihastha, a householder, can also reach Krishna, provided he becomes a pure devotee without material desires.
>
> [*Srimad-Bhagavatam* 7.15.67, purport]

Engagement in such worship of the Deity, under the direction of a bona fide spiritual master, will greatly help the householders to purify their very existence and make rapid progress in spiritual knowledge.

[*Srimad-Bhagavatam* 2.3.22, purport]

More about this principle of Spiritual Growth and Progress can be found in:

- Chapter 3: Roles of the Husband and Wife in the Vaishnava Community
- Chapter 7: Spiritual Parenting
- Chapter 9: A Balanced and Sustainable Marriage
- Chapter 10: Giving Back: Making a Social Contribution

PRINCIPLE #3 – Spiritual Equality / Material Difference

Recognizing Differences between Men and Women – Men and women have general physical and psychological differences that we need to acknowledge as practical realities, while avoiding unhealthy and rigid stereotypes. There just isn't one mold that fits everyone! In Vedic culture we recognize that a wife's submission and service to her husband is highly revered. Women require protection and security especially when caring for children and in old age. Srila Prabhupada discusses the need of the husband to feel the respect and confidence of all the family members. Men generally like to feel "in charge." Keeping this in mind, it is important that husband and wife discuss what roles are appropriate for them in marriage within a Krishna conscious context and consider the time, place, and circumstance.

Understanding the Concept of Time, Place, and Circumstance – The Gaudiya Vaishnava philosophy offers a clear conceptual model by which we can understand time, place, and circumstance on many levels. Issues such as gender expectations, women's place in the workforce, and normative family roles vary greatly across our vast ISKCON world. Devotees come from many backgrounds. Our past experiences, cultural norms, professional identities, and length of time in devotional service may influence how a couple defines their relationship in service to each other. In inter-cultural marriages, these negotiations and clarifications are especially important. As with any aspect of spiritual life, marital relationships in Krishna consciousness will evolve, change, and mature over time.

Integrating Material and Spiritual Identities – Householders are advised, as much as possible, to integrate their material and spiritual identities. Although our spiritual identity is ultimately most important, it is essential in spiritual life to cultivate self-understanding on a material level as well. In other words, *understand the present body at the present time.* We have to work with the material body and our material circumstances to cultivate spiritual consciousness. A marriage partner can be a great support in this regard.

Spiritual Equality in Marriage – Both men and women have equal rights to practice Krishna consciousness and to develop their individual relationships with Krishna. However, in marriage there is the added advantage of having husband and wife assist and support each other in their devotional services. According to Vaishnava philosophy, service to the devotee – which includes service to our devotee marriage partner – is the highest service and most pleasing to Lord Krishna.

What did Srila Prabhupada teach us about spiritual equality and material difference?

> To be either a woman or a man only involves one's bodily dress. The soul in nature is actually the marginal energy of the Supreme Lord.
>
> [*Srimad-Bhagavatam* 3.31.41, purport]

> A man's psychology and woman's psychology are different. As constituted by bodily frame, a man always wants to be superior to his wife.
>
> [*Srimad-Bhagavatam* 3.23.2, purport]

> Women in general, being very simple at heart, can very easily take to Krishna consciousness, and when they develop love of Krishna they can easily get liberation from the clutches of maya [illusion], which are very difficult for even so-called intelligent and learned men to surpass.
>
> [*Krishna Book,* Chapter 23: Delivering the Wives of the Brahmanas]

> Since both the boys and the girls are being trained to become preachers, those girls are not ordinary girls but are as good as their brothers who are preaching Krishna consciousness. Therefore, to engage both boys and girls in fully transcendental activities is a policy intended to spread the Krishna consciousness movement.
>
> [*Chaitanya-charitamrita, Adi* 7.31-32, purport]

More about this principle of Spiritual Equality and Material Difference can be found in:

- Chapter 3: Roles of the Husband and Wife in the Vaishnava Community
- Chapter 6: Affection and Physical Intimacy: The "Hot Potato"

PRINCIPLE #4 – Positive and Realistic Vision

Family Life in the Material World – There is a crisis in family life in this world. High rates of divorce and broken families are a result of putting "I, me and mine" above everything else. Commitment and responsibility in marriage are increasingly attributes of past generations. As spiritual practitioners, we need to enter the grihastha ashrama with the correct attitude. Most importantly, devotees need to acknowledge that cultivating strong and healthy spiritual marriage is an on-going process and to recognize that there will be challenges along the way.

Realistic Expectations About Our Partners – Devotees should avoid having unrealistic expectations about their partner. It is unlikely that your spouse will be a perfect Draupadi or Arjuna; instead, we should remember that although we may have faults, we are all endeavoring on the spiritual path.

Avoiding Negative Influences on Household Life – Devotees should be careful to avoid negative influences and inappropriate personal or social paradigms such as, "I am falling into the deep, dark well of household life because I am such a bad, fallen devotee and cannot control my senses." This is not a helpful way of thinking and will be very damaging to your relationship, which in turn negatively impacts the devotee community. Grihastha life is a spiritual path recommended by sadhu, shastra, and guru. This alone should give you enthusiasm to learn, grow, and progress in this ashrama.

Self Evaluation before Marriage – Before entering the grihastha ashrama, it is important to be self-reflective. Try to hold yourself up to the measure by asking such questions as "What are my qualifications as a spouse in a spiritual marriage? What will I contribute to this spiritual relationship?" Together with your prospective spouse, you can make short-term and long-term goals. Strategic marriage planning, while maintaining a mood of dependence on Lord Krishna, is very helpful and can clarify many issues in a new relationship. Premarital counseling is effective; we highly recommend it.

Role of Elders in Grihastha Life – Traditionally in Vedic culture, the role of elders is very important. Extended families provide wisdom and support. However, many of us do not have parents, grandparents, or siblings who are engaged in spiritual life. In that case, we have to rely on senior grihastha couples and other trusted devotees for guidance and support.

What did Srila Prabhupada teach us about positive and realistic vision?

> You have asked if I found it difficult to carry on devotional service when in my household life, and yes, I did…You try to take care of Lord Jagannatha as far as possible after doing your household duties, but you should be strict only in completing the 16 rounds of chanting. That will save you from all discrepancies. As a householder even there

is some flaws in following the rules and regulations, it doesn't matter. You should try your best and…Krishna will help you. If you keep your heart in that attitude, that you want to become a pure and sincere devotee…Krishna will help you.

[Letter to Malati, 23 November 1968]

The grihasthas, they become sometimes distressed. The grihastha ashrama means unless there is Krishna or full consciousness of Krishna, it is simply miserable, simply miserable. *Duhkhalayam asasvatam.*[1] Simply working hard day and night, then there is, child is sick, then wife is not satisfied, the servant is not satisfied… So many things, problem. But if there is Krishna in the center, [all the] problems will be solved…That is grihastha ashrama.

[Lecture on *Bhagavad-gita* 1.31 – London, 24 July 1973]

There are two words in Sanskrit language. One is *grha-stha*, and one is *grha-vrata* or *grha-medhi* [materialistic family life]. Grihastha means grihastha ashrama…Those who are conversant with Vedic language, they know. Ashrama means something in connection with God. That is called ashrama. So grihastha ashrama means one may live with family, children, wife, children, friends – that's all right. Live. Whatever life is suitable for you, you accept. But you change Krishna consciousness. Cultivate Krishna consciousness. That is ashrama.

[Lecture on *Srimad-Bhagavatam* 7.5.22-30 – London, 8 September 1971]

More about this principle of Positive and Realistic Vision can be found in:

- Chapter 2: Ready or Not, Here I Come: Preparation for Marriage

- Chapter 3: Roles of the Husband and Wife in the Vaishnava Community

- Chapter 5: Krishna's Economics: Spiritualize Your Wealth

- Chapter 8: Marriage Under Attack: Dealing with Serious Conflict, Separation, and Divorce

PRINCIPLE #5 – Mutual Respect and Appreciation

Importance of Mutual Respect – Respect and appreciation for others are basic Vaishnava values. Respect and appreciation go hand in hand with humility and a service attitude. When both partners honor these values, strong, loving, and caring relationships flourish. In the absence of respect and appreciation, relationships inevitably quickly deteriorate.

Appreciating the Little Things – We can openly appreciate our spouse even for the routine duties they perform each day. In this way, we can develop intimacy and closeness without falling into the trap of over-familiarity. In other words, we will not be as likely to take our spouse for granted. Celebrate the devotional service of your partner and always show respect and appreciation for your partner's contributions. As we will see in later chapters, this is the key to maintaining peace and harmony.

Mutual Protection for Grihasthas – As grihasthas we should develop a sense of mutual protection as well. The material world is a dangerous place, and spiritual life is not always easy. Of course, according to circumstances, protection may take different forms and mean different things to each partner. Protection and support in all facets of one's life are valuable assets of grihastha life.

What did Srila Prabhupada teach us about mutual respect and appreciation?

> Suppose if you love somebody... You simply take from him, but you don't give. Oh, do you think it is very good? No. It is not good. That is not love. That is exploitation. If I go on simply taking from you, and if I don't offer you anything, that is simply exploitation. So love means you must take, you must give. *Dadati pratigrhnati bhunkte, bhunkte bhojayate.*
>
> [Lecture on *Bhagavad-gita* 9.2-5 – New York, 23 November 1966]

> Everyone should praise another's service to the Lord and not be proud of his own service. This is the way of Vaishnava thinking, Vaikuntha thinking. There may be rivalries and apparent competition between servants in performing service, but in the Vaikuntha planets the service of another servant is appreciated, not condemned. This is Vaikuntha competition. There is no question of enmity between servants. Everyone should be allowed to render service to the Lord to the best of his ability, and everyone should appreciate the service of others. Such are the activities of Vaikuntha. Since everyone is a servant, everyone is on the same platform and is allowed to serve the Lord according to his ability.
>
> [*Srimad-Bhagavatam* 7.5.12, purport]

More about this principle of Mutual Respect and Appreciation can be found in:

- Chapter 3: Roles of the Husband and Wife in the Vaishnava Community

- Chapter 4: Let's Talk About It: Open and Honest Communication

- Chapter 6: Affection and Intimacy: The "Hot Potato"

- Chapter 8: Marriage Under Attack: Dealing with Serious Conflict, Separation, and Divorce

PRINCIPLE #6 – Commitment and Dedication

Romantic Love vs. Genuine Love – Devotees must practice commitment and dedication in Krishna conscious life in order to continue to grow spiritually. It is the same in married life. Hard times are inevitable, but with unshakable determination and commitment, almost any challenge can be surmounted. We are conditioned to think of marriage in terms of the romantic love reflected in movies and novels. These popularized concepts may be foolish and unrealistic. Genuine love and affection do not happen automatically with the impact of Cupid's arrow. They are developed through dedicated service and the cultivation of mutual respect and admiration. As in any devotee relationship, spiritual intimacy and closeness develop as a result of serving in Krishna consciousness together.

Seeking Help from Others in Difficult Times – Sometimes, devotees need the help of others when facing difficult times. This should be sought out when needed and given when requested. Divorce should be avoided at all costs as a general principle. However in situations of chronic abuse, Srila Prabhupada did allow his disciples to leave their marriages. Again, senior devotees or counselors should be consulted when facing such difficult decisions.

What did Srila Prabhupada teach us about commitment and dedication?

> Formerly husband and wife used to live together peacefully throughout their whole lives.
>
> [*Srimad-Bhagavatam* 3.21.15, purport]

> Yes. Wife and husband, once combined, that is for life. There is no question of separation, in all circumstances. Either in distress or in happiness, there is no question of separation.
>
> [Arrival Address – London, 11 September 1969]

> It is not that a chaste woman should be like a slave while her husband is *naradhama*, the lowest of men. Although the duties of a woman are different from those of a man, a chaste woman is not meant to serve a fallen husband. If her husband is fallen, it is recommended that she give up his association. Giving up the association of her husband

does not mean, however, that a woman should marry again and thus indulge in prostitution. If a chaste woman unfortunately marries a husband who is fallen, she should live separately from him. Similarly, a husband can separate himself from a woman who is not chaste according to the description of the shastra.

[*Srimad-Bhagavatam* 7.11.28, purport]

More about this principle of Commitment and Dedication can be found in:

- Chapter 2: Ready or Not, Here I Come: Preparation for Marriage
- Chapter 6: Affection and Physical Intimacy: The "Hot Potato"
- Chapter 8: Marriage Under Attack: Dealing with Serious Conflict, Separation, and Divorce

PRINCIPLE #7 – Open and Honest Communication

Key to Marital Harmony – Open and honest communication is a key to peaceful and happy marriage. Even with a busy schedule, it is important to set aside time for heart to heart communications with your spouse and children. In spiritual life, we understand that revealing the heart and mind in trust and listening to others in confidence are important exchanges between Vaishnavas. This is particularly important within family units where love and trust is built by open communication and service. Maintaining open dialogues with your spouse, particularly regarding such sensitive issues as intimacy, sex life, and financial matters, is extremely important in building trust, cooperation, and confidence.

Communication: a Skill to Be Learned and Practiced – Effective communication is a skill that can be learned and practiced. Many marriages have greatly benefitted when the couple has taken time to develop these skills with the help of qualified counselors or marriage educators.

What did Srila Prabhupada teach us about open and honest communication?

Offering gifts in charity, accepting charitable gifts, revealing one's mind in confidence, inquiring confidentially, accepting *prasada* and offering *prasada* are the six symptoms of love shared by one devotee and another.

[*Nectar of Instruction* 4]

Guhyam akhyati prcchati. And you disclose your mind; there is no secrecy between the lover and the beloved. And the other party also discloses. In this way, love becomes manifest.

[Lecture on *Chaitanya-charitamrita, Madhya* 20.101, Washington, DC, 6 July 1976]

More about this principle of Open and Honest Communication can be found in:

- Chapter 3: Let's Talk About It: Open and Honest Communication
- Chapter 6: Affection and Physical Intimacy: The "Hot Potato"
- Chapter 8: Marriage Under Attack: Dealing with Serious Conflict, Separation, and Divorce

PRINCIPLE #8 – Personal and Social Responsibility

Our Service to Society – Grihasthas, by definition, are truly the servants of society. Householders have the duty to financially support the temples as well as the other ashramas. Historically and philosophically, brahmacharis and sannyasis have a limited financial base and are dependent on the grihasthas for their material well-being. Grihasthas should also provide leadership and management so that the brahmacharis and sannyasis are free to travel, teach, and study. In turn, the renounced ashramas provide the householders with spiritual inspiration, education, and association. Although ISKCON is not presently able to function fully in this Vedic model, the grihastha devotees are gradually assuming such responsibilities as our young movement matures. The goal of many householders is to serve in these ways.

Householders as Examples to the Greater Society – Grihasthas, by their good work and moral and spiritual lifestyle, can become an example for the wider society to follow. They should demonstrate integrity, responsibility, family cohesiveness, leadership and other exemplary qualities. These qualities are very attractive and bring others to Krishna consciousness. People in general are looking for loving, caring, and stable family life in a spiritual context.

Opportunity to Make Advancement in Grihastha Life – Grihastha ashrama is an opportunity to become mature and steady in spiritual life. Taking such responsibility is essential for overcoming negative emotions and in dealing with the pitfalls of low self-esteem, discouragement, or feelings of failure. It is an ashrama where the devotee can truly express himself or herself in spiritual, material, and professional life while making great advancement in Krishna consciousness by dovetailing all aspects of life in Krishna's service.

What did Srila Prabhupada teach us about personal and social responsibility?

The main duties of a householder are to give shelter to all living entities and perform sacrifices.

[*Srimad-Bhagavatam* 11.18.42]

I am very much pleased to know that you are trying to set a fine example to your young son, Joseph, and your good wife. It is the duty of our students who are married men to train both their wife and children in devotional service to the Supreme Lord. The easiest program is that you add to your daily schedule a *kirtana* chanting of Hare Krishna ma-ha-mantra both in the evening and the morning with your family and after chanting you can read something from our *Bhagavad Gita As It Is* or *Krishna Book* or our other literatures. You are already offering service to Lord Jagannatha and offering Him some nicely prepared fruits, milk, sweet smelling flowers and incense. That is the way for householders.

[Letter to Ben, 22 November 1970]

One section of people, the householders, they have to maintain the three other divisions. We have divided the society into four divisions: brahmachari, grihastha, vanaprastha, and sannyasa. Only the grihasthas are allowed to make money, to earn money.

[Lecture on *Srimad-Bhagavatam* 7.6.6-9
– Montreal, 23 June 1968]

Advaita Acharya set an ideal example for all householder devotees in His reception of Lord Chaitanya Mahaprabhu and His devotees and in His execution of a daily festival at His home. If one has the proper means and wealth, he should occasionally invite the devotees of Lord Chaitanya who are engaged in preaching all over the world and hold a festival at home simply by distributing *prasadam* and talking about Krishna during the day and holding congregational chanting for at least three hours in the evening. This procedure must be adopted in all centers of the Krishna consciousness movement. Thus they will daily perform *sankirtana-yajna*.

[*Chaitanya-charitamrita, Madhya* 3.203, purport]

Someone might argue that since Prahlada Maharaja, even though very old, was attached to his family, and specifically to his grandson Bali Maharaja, how could he be an ideal example? Therefore this verse uses the word *prasantah*. A devotee is always sober. He is never disturbed by any conditions. Even if a devotee remains in grihastha life and does not renounce material possessions, he should still be understood to be *prasanta*, sober, because of his pure devotion to the Lord.

[*Srimad-Bhagavatam* 8.19.2, purport]

More about this principle of Personal and Social Responsibility can be found in:

- Chapter 5: Krishna's Economics: Spiritualizing Your Wealth
- Chapter 10: Giving Back: Making a Social Contribution

PRINCIPLE #9 – Economic Development and Prosperity

Generating Wealth – An important householder duty is to generate wealth and prosperity by ethical means. This is because giving in charity is an essential duty for the grihastha ashrama. In this spirit, householders should financially support and promote activities such as establishing and maintaining temples, distributing books and *prasadam,* and other outreach programs.

Avoiding Poverty Mentality – Grihastha ashrama should <u>not</u> be an ashrama of poverty and great material austerity. Poverty, as well as overindulgence, can be an impediment to spiritual life. Creating wealth can have enormous benefits both for individual family stability and promoting Krishna consciousness. This is not incompatible with the mood of simple living and high thinking, not striving for material opulence beyond what is strictly necessary. True renunciation is to offer the results of one's work in Krishna conscious service. This is the highest service for householders.

What did Srila Prabhupada teach us about economic development and prosperity?

If by chance or by the grace of the Lord more money comes, it should be properly engaged for the Krishna consciousness movement. One should not be eager to earn more money simply for sensual pleasure.

[*Srimad-Bhagavatam* 7.14, Chapter Summary]

Any householder, he requires some deposit in the bank for emergency. That is, of course, allowed for householders. But just for us, we are sannyasi; we are renounced order of... We haven't got to accumulate any money. You see? That is the system of Indian philosophy. But those who are householder, family men, they may have some deposit for emergency.

[Lecture on *Bhagavad-gita* 2.46-47 – New York, 28 March 1966]

More about this principle of Economic Development and Prosperity can be found in:

• Chapter 5: Krishna's Economics: Spiritualizing Your Wealth

PRINCIPLE #10 – Focus on Children's Welfare

Protection and Guidance of Children in Krishna Consciousness – Srila Prabhupada instructed his disciples about the sacred duty of taking proper care of our children. He said that these children are gifts from Krishna and must be protected and guided in Krishna conscious life. The care of children should not be neglected for any reason. It is the primary devotional service for a parent. Protection means more than providing for material needs and bodily safety. Protection also means to protect them from material illusion by inspiring them in devotional service and life in Krishna consciousness. Protection includes providing for legitimate and essential material needs while teaching children that material overindulgence will not bring more than temporary happiness. Modeling and celebrating simple living and high thinking is a great gift for a child.

Community Responsibility Towards All Children – Parents also have a duty to all children in the community and not just to their own offspring. It is the responsibility of a community to be alert and proactive in order to prevent all forms of child abuse. Parents should also provide and fund educational opportunities for children in a Krishna conscious environment and help foster an overall environment of protection and affection in the community of devotees. Relevant and accessible community activities involving children are important in order to foster a sense of belonging and a taste for devotional life. This is especially important for teenagers who often question and challenge their own parents, but may listen to other devotees.

Importance of Learning Parenting Skills – Senior devotees or counselors can often provide useful information, enhance parenting skills, or provide support to parents. Everyone faces challenges as a parent. Accepting training or assistance is important and sometimes necessary.

Children Learn What They Live – Above all, we should also remember that children are very intuitive – they learn what they live. Hypocrisy is damaging to children's faith in Krishna consciousness. As parents and other authority figures, we must "practice what we preach" and "walk our talk" in order to inspire the next generation.

What did Srila Prabhupada teach us about focus on children's welfare?

> These children are given to us by Krishna, they are Vaishnavas, and we must be very careful to protect them. These are not ordinary children, they are Vaikuntha children, and we are very fortunate we can give them chance to advance further in Krishna consciousness. That is very great responsibility, do not neglect it or be confused. Your duty is very clear.

[Letter to Arundhati, 30 July 1972]

I consider this *gurukula* school to be one of our most important aspects of this movement and it should be given all serious consideration by the members. If we are able to make a whole generation of our children into fine Krishna conscious preachers that will be the glory of our movement and the glory of your country as well. But if we neglect somehow or other and if we lose even one Vaishnava, that is very great loss.

[Letter to Stoka Krishna, 20 June 1972]

The profits from the businesses should first go to support *gurukula* and balance may be given for the local Temple's maintenance. Grihasthas can do business.

[Letter to Jayatirtha, 22 January 1976]

More about this principle of Focus on Children's Welfare can be found in:

• Chapter 7: Sacred Parenting: What Krishna Conscious Parents Want to Know

PRINCIPLE #11 – Family Love and Affection

Vaishnava Family Affection is Natural – It is natural to have affection for others and especially for other Vaishnava*s*. Family ties are not necessarily impediments to Krishna consciousness. In fact, they can be very instrumental to the success of a devotee by providing association, obligation, and stability in life. Being a devotee does not mean that we have to stifle or negate natural affection for our family members. All members of the family need to feel loved, valued, protected, and appreciated. Children need to be given affection, attention, and personal time by both parents. Spouses need to express love and affection for each other through mutual service and appreciation. The family unit is where moral values are taught and where the spiritual and cultural heritage of the society is passed on. Without love and trust, children will be less likely to be inclined to accept their parent's values including Krishna consciousness.

Role of Extended Family and Community – Extended family and community are also vital in providing a sense of belonging and security. They can be instrumental in ensuring that family members stay strong in their commitments, and they can provide support and assistance in times of difficulty and stress. A strong extended family or devotee community promotes both social responsibility and solidarity. There is strength in numbers.

What did Srila Prabhupada teach us about family love and affection?

> This reciprocation of service and love between husband and wife is the ideal of a householder's life.
>
> [*Srimad-Bhagavatam* 3.23.1, purport]

"My dear beautiful wife, you know that because we are householders we are always busy in many household affairs and long for a time when we can enjoy some joking words between us. That is our ultimate gain in household life." Actually, householders work very hard day and night, but all fatigue of the day's labor is minimized as soon as they meet, husband and wife together, and enjoy life in many ways. Lord Krishna wanted to exhibit Himself as being like an ordinary householder who delights himself by exchanging joking words with his wife.

> [*Krishna Book*, Chapter 60, Talks Between Krishna and Rukmini]

Naradaji saw that Lord Krishna was engaged as an affectionate father petting His small children.

> [*Krishna Book,* Chapter 69, The Great Sage Narada Visits the Different Homes of Lord Krishna]

More about this principle of Family Love and Affection can be found in:

- Chapter 6: Affection and Physical Intimacy: The "Hot Potato"

- Chapter 7: Sacred Parenting: What Krishna Conscious Parents Want to Know

PRINCIPLE #12 – Regulated, Balanced, and Exemplary Lifestyle

Regulation and Strong Sadhana – Regulation is an important feature of devotional life. This is especially true for householders who are balancing many responsibilities such as sadhana, childcare, employment, devotional services, and spiritual outreach activities. When devotees move into the grihastha ashrama, they should anticipate changes in their routine. Life may suddenly seem more complicated and can even feel overwhelming. Maintaining strong sadhana will always make all the other efforts happen more smoothly.

Simple Living, High Thinking – Husband and wife negotiate and establish their own lifestyles, with reference to Krishna conscious principles and values, considering their individual natures, needs, and backgrounds. Unlike the other ashramas, in the grihastha ashrama there is latitude for individual initiative, creativity, and independence. In this regard however, we need to understand that household life is meant to regulate sense-enjoyment. A householder should maintain healthy attitudes towards sense-enjoyment, demonstrating neither strong attraction nor inappropriate aversion. The goal is simple living and high thinking in a regulated, balanced, and exemplary lifestyle.

Remaining Steady in the Face of Difficulties – It is advised that all couples plan carefully before entering marriage. Premarital counseling or consultation with senior devotees is a necessary step. As one goes through the stages of grihastha life with a growing family, financial and career development, and community involvement, it is advisable to periodically step back and conscientiously take stock of priorities and goals.

As in any ashrama, grihastha devotees will likely face major challenges during times of change and adjustment. The birth of a child, the beginning of a new job, dealing with illness, and times of financial stress can all feel overwhelming. At such times, the challenge of maintaining a balanced and exemplary lifestyle can seem almost impossible. Recognize that sometimes even the most sincere and strict devotees will have times of difficulty in maintaining all of their spiritual and material obligations. At these times, married devotees need to be understanding and supportive of each other. Normal life will return in due course of time. Taking shelter of trusted devotee couples is always helpful as well.

Modeling a Happy, Healthy Spiritual Lifestyle – Recreational and social life is important for grihasthas. They should develop suitable means to be active community members by organizing and participating in spiritually based programs and social gatherings. Suitable outreach activities with those outside of the devotee community are often an integral part of both personal growth and spiritual advancement. Providing an example of a happy, healthy spiritual lifestyle helps others become attracted to Krishna consciousness. Role models, especially in the form of successful grihasthas, are very much needed within the larger society.

What did Srila Prabhupada teach us about a regulated, balanced, and exemplary lifestyle?

> He who is regulated in his habits of eating, sleeping, recreation and work can mitigate all material pains by practicing the yoga system.
>
> [*Bhagavad-gita* 6.17]

> One must find some time for hearing *Srimad-Bhagavatam* and *Bhagavad-gita*. This is Vedic culture. One should work eight hours at the most to earn his livelihood, and either in the afternoon or in the evening a householder should associate with devotees to hear about the incarnations of Krishna and His activities and thus be gradually liberated from the clutches of maya.
>
> [*Srimad-Bhagavatam* 7.14.3-4, purport]

More about this principle of Regulated, Balanced, and Exemplary Lifestyle can be found in:

- Chapter 7: Sacred Parenting: What Krishna Conscious Parents Want to Know

- Chapter 9: A Balanced and Sustainable Marriage

- Chapter 10: Giving Back: Making a Social Contribution

Conclusion

The more you keep these principles and values in mind as you read through the chapters of this book, the more you will benefit. We sincerely hope that by studying and putting into practice the various practical applications as they are presented, these Twelve Principles for Successful Krishna Conscious Family Life will truly become an integral support for your spiritual growth. Hare Krishna!

About the Author

PRAHARANA DEVI DASI (Pam McFarlane, BSc, MSW, RSW) was initiated by His Divine Grace A. C. Bhaktivedanta Swami Prabhupada in 1972 on Radhastami in Toronto, Canada. She served for many years in Toronto as a *pujari*, on *sankirtana,* and performing administrative work. In 1976, she was married and subsequently had three children, Abhay Charan, Remuna, and Krishna Keli. Finding herself a single parent in 1988 and needing financial stability to support her family, she returned to university, earning a master's degree in social work. She has been employed as a clinical social worker for the past 20 years. As well as serving on the management committee of Govinda's Restaurant in Toronto, mentoring the youth on the Toronto temple council, and working with the GVT, Praharana devi dasi continues to serve as the Regional Secretary for Canada on both the North American GBC Group and the Canadian National Council.

Chapter 2 Ready or Not: Here I Come: Preparation for Marriage

Uttama devi dasi

In this chapter you will learn:

✓ Characteristics of One Who is Ready for Marriage

✓ Healthy Expectations for Marriage

✓ How to Recognize if You and Your Partner are Compatible

✓ Red Flag Warnings

✓ Needed Blessings

Bhaktin French Fry using maha flower to pick a mate.

Principles Highlighted in this Chapter

- Positive and Realistic Vision
- Commitment and Dedication

To Marry or Not to Marry...

I married when I was 17. According to statistics, I had very poor odds for long term marital success. By Krishna's grace, I've been married for more than 40 years. If you are a teenager preparing for marriage, even I would probably think that you were either impetuous or pregnant. I ran into a friend a year after I was married, and she immediately asked me about my baby. She just assumed that I'd had a "shotgun" wedding. I didn't. Fortunately, my husband and I enjoyed a compatibility that more than compensated for the risk of marrying so young.

Most people eventually feel the need to get married. It was Srila Bhaktivinoda Thakura who recommended the grihastha ashrama as the safest ashrama for progressing in spiritual life.[1] Yet despite all of this, because we all have seen so many unhealthy marriages around us, you may be hesitant to tread the marriage path. At least, you may feel a little unsure how to proceed. When the present divorce rate in the developed countries is over 50%, it is understandable that many people are unsure about marriage, even when they are "madly in love." The purpose of this chapter is to help you understand some of the complexities involved in choosing a suitable marriage partner. I will also discuss how to be proactive in preparing yourself for a healthy, happy, and long-lasting marriage relationship.

Getting Your Own House in Order

Are You Ready for Marriage? – What determines our readiness for marriage? Is it merely the desire for relationships with the opposite sex? Is it our biological clock? Is it convenience? Is it our dharma? In our devotee community, we have seen what happens when a person suppresses his or her desire to be married. Such a person may manifest symptoms such as moroseness, unexplained illness, anxiety, withdrawal from one's usual association, increased fault finding, excessive "preaching" that demeans the opposite sex, or perhaps leaving the movement altogether.

How Supportive is Your Environment? – Hopefully, you are in a supportive environment that acknowledges your needs – assisting you in the transition from single life to married life – rather than in one that minimizes or even ridicules your decision to get married. If those around you view marriage as a sort of compromise for persons who couldn't "make it," or as a "fall down" into the deep dark well of family life, you may enter into the grihastha ashrama with a sense of shame. You may even harbor resentment towards your marriage partner for being an accomplice to the "crime of marriage." If this is the case, you should either forsake that negative association or forsake the idea of marriage.

Positive Examples from Scripture – *Srimad-Bhagavatam* relates how Kardama Muni prayed to the Lord for a suitable partner.[2] The Lord was personally present, so we may wonder why Kardama Muni did not ask instead to be taken immediately to the spiritual realm. Srila Prabhupada, Founder-*Acharya* of the International Society for Krishna Consciousness, comments that Kardama Muni could ascertain that he was not yet competent for liberation, but that he could advance to that platform with the help of a good wife. As the saying goes, God helps those who help themselves. Krishna was very pleased to make suitable arrangements for him.

Seeing Marriage as a Positive Step Favorable for Your Spiritual Growth – Let us assume that you are open to the possibilities of a real, Krishna conscious marriage and view it as a joyful rite of passage – a mature commitment to a responsible life, favorable for your spiritual growth. If you can tell yourself with 100% conviction that the grihastha ashrama is an honorable institution with as much spiritual integrity as the other three ashramas, you are well on your way to the next step – seeking a suitable candidate as your future spouse.

> As a fort commander very easily conquers invading plunderers, by taking shelter of a wife one can conquer the senses, which are unconquerable in the other social orders.
>
> *Srimad-Bhagavatam* 3.14.20

Are you really ready? – Most of the qualities that you should look for in a partner are also qualities that you should possess. As you read on, be introspective and see if there are skills you could learn, attitudes you could change, or values you could aspire to live by.

Marriage is Not a Cure for Your Personal Unhappiness – Before moving to the next topic, I want to emphasize that you should examine your own motivation for wanting to get married. It is best not to have the expectation that the other person is responsible for your happiness. If you are not a happy person, work on dealing with your personal issues before looking for a partner. If you have unhealthy emotional needs, you may develop relationship patterns that attempt to resolve interpersonally what you can only resolve within yourself. Unhealthy emotional needs may cause you to unload unrealistic expectations on your marriage partner, thus placing an unfair burden on him or her. A marriage partner is not an antidote for your personal unhappiness.

Marriage is Not a Cure for Less-Than-Ideal Sadhana – Over the years, some women have expressed to me their desire for a really dedicated spiritual partner to help them improve their sadhana, their spiritual practices. Association is certainly a key element for good sadhana, but ultimately the responsibility for spiritual life rests with the individual.

Know Your Family Issues and Actively Work on Them – Even when you are working on your personal issues, and consciously think you want a healthy relationship, there are important patterns to examine that can cause marital discord. People from unhealthy families are often unconsciously driven to seek relationships with the same unhealthy, dysfunctional patterns they grew up around. In Western psychology, this is viewed as an attempt to fix the relationship they had in childhood. For example, a woman may repeatedly marry abusive men (like her overbearing father), or a man may repeatedly seek out women who are emotionally distant and unavailable (like his unfeeling mother) as a subconscious attempt to recreate the situation, fix it, and attain closure. Better to find closure first, and then move on to a healthy situation. From the viewpoint of Vedic psychology, we understand this to be the unresolved karmic lessons from past actions, good or bad, continuing to teach us what we need to learn to progress on our spiritual journey.

For Example – Janis grew up in an alcoholic family. Her mother was alcoholic and her father often stayed away from home on business trips. Janis took on a lot of her mother's responsibilities – caring for younger children and worrying about bills getting paid. When she was older and in relationships, she always seemed to end up with guys who were irresponsible, had addiction problems, or weren't good at handling their money. Now that she has become a devotee, she wants to get married but is afraid she will attract a similar person into her life. She decides to get counseling to understand why this is happening. She works on her past. She comes to understand how her identity is tied up in rescuing others – she doesn't have a sense of who she is without this. She realizes she could easily misapply the philosophy of compassion. Once she recognizes her patterns, she identifies healthy behaviors and puts them into practice.

Heal Old Wounds before Marriage – Self realization includes understanding your conditioned identity. Don't think your negative conditioning is "just the way I am," but endeavor to improve yourself through introspection, professional help if necessary, and intense spiritual practice and prayer. The more you understand yourself and your prospective spouse, the better.

Not that we have to be perfect saints to be marital partners, but at least we should be sincerely endeavoring to be the best devotees we can.

Again, I am stressing the need to release and heal old wounds as much possible before marriage. Then you may work to help one another in marriage, and not be just reliving old karmic patterns.

Conversely, be hesitant to get involved with someone if they haven't sorted out or are at least working on their own personal issues. In short, you should be the best person you can be. Then, on that platform, you can look for a suitable, like-minded partner. The more emotionally stable you are, the better your chances of finding a like-minded person and the stronger your foundation for a lasting relationship.

Expectations

Know What You Want — Before you begin looking for something, you need to be clear exactly what it is you are trying to find. It sounds obvious, yet there are many people who continually make bad choices in relationships. Often this is caused by accelerated attachments in new relationships, also known as being blinded by love.

To avoid this pitfall, it is a good idea to be clear what you expect out of a relationship. Being consciously aware of your expectations and making sure that those expectations are realistic is a solid foundation from which to start.

The key here is that the more we clarify the values, principles, and needs that are important to us, the easier it will be for Krishna to help us. Vague goals will take us to an uncertain destination or nowhere at all.

For example, I have a friend who really wanted to be in a relation-ship. Even though she is a devotee of Krishna, she decided to pray to Lord Shiva for a husband (following in the footsteps of the gopis, I suppose). In her prayers, she focused on three particular qualities that she wanted her would-be husband to possess. She soon ended up married to a devotee with those particular qualities but nothing else. Consequently, she is not happy in her relationship. In other words, she got what she asked for, but what she asked for was not a complete inventory of all that she needed or wanted.

> EXERCISE: Before you commit to someone, write down the top ten qualities you most desire in a prospective partner. Extend that list to include sub-qualities and desirable behavior patterns. Then write down five behavior traits that you probably could not tolerate in a partner. Some of the items on this list may change over time, but at least it will help you to clearly understand your values and expectations. Make your list as extensive as possible. Also consider: How many of these traits – good or bad – do you possess?

In addition, be careful about succumbing to the feeling of desperation to find someone and then settling for someone you intuitively know is wrong – trying to fit a square peg in a round hole. This is common, especially if you have low self-esteem or feel your biological clock ticking.

Positive and Realistic Expectations are the Key

Choose a Devotee of the Lord — The first and most important consideration when looking for a spouse is whether or not they are a devotee of the Lord. This is validated by sadhu, shastra, and guru. However, I have found that devotees are sometimes too simplistic in applying this principle. They seem to forget that there are all sorts of devotees situated on different levels of consciousness. Does the devotee you want to marry have similar goals? What kinds of devotional activities appeal to him or her?

Certainly all devotees are to be respected as the best among the general crowd, but not every devotee will practice their spiritual life in a manner that is compatible with yours. Perhaps a major contributing factor to the high divorce rate among western Vaishnavas is that in the past we did not take our individual spiritual dispositions sufficiently into account when choosing a partner.

A feeling of really knowing a person may come somewhat from the shared values of devotees. This kind of assumption can override seeing potential incompatible personality differences. The significant point here is that you should take the time to examine your expectations and your personal values for a relationship.

Seeking Help – Working on the list mentioned in the exercise box on the previous page can help you ascertain your expectations, values, and goals. The Grihastha Vision Team recommends that you seek the help of a Vaishnava marriage and family professional, whenever possible, to assist you in working through this kind of in-depth examination.

Beginning the Search in Earnest – After you get your own emotional house in order, and after you establish your expectations, you can begin your search in earnest. To help you determine whether or not you can get along with someone in a long term marriage relationship, it is important to consider such things as family of origin, personality, experiences, and education. It is also a good idea to look for any "red flags" that may suggest destructive behavior patterns.

At some point in this deliberation, you should seek the advice and blessings of family members and other older devotees whose judgment you value.

Finally, be aware of those qualities which, according to the experts, are invaluable for long term marital success.

Fundamental Character

Look for Compassion – In the Third Canto of the *Srimad-Bhagavatam*, the Lord instructs Kardama Muni about grihastha life. Among other things, He tells Kardama Muni that the primary responsibility of a grihastha is to be compassionate and liberal to others.

Compassion is essentially the opposite of selfishness. Compassion is the ability to be sensitive to the needs of others and the will to assist another person in achieving what is best for them. Compassion can contribute more to a relationship than romantic love alone ever can.

Lack of compassion is regarded as the root cause of abuse in relationships.[3] If we expect to have caring relationships, we should have the ability to compassionately see what is best for the other person and to do what we can to help them achieve it. In other words, selfish people do not enjoy happy marriages; compassionate people do.

Look for Kindness – Other desirable qualities to look for in a potential spouse are kindness and flexibility. Kindness ranks high in surveys across many cultures as a quality which people deeply appreciate in their spouse. High levels of kindness and flexibility in a relationship lead to high levels of effective communication and positive conflict resolution. Look for someone who is kind and flexible, and practice being flexible and kind yourself.

Look for Emotional Maturity – Find a partner who is emotionally mature. Emotional maturity is characterized by calmness and high self esteem. Studies have shown that emotionally immature people tend to bring a lot of criticism and defensiveness to their relationships. Criticism and defensiveness between couples generally leads to relationship instability, pain, and withdrawal. Maturity involves knowing one's values and having the integrity to live by them.

Compatible Family Background

Positive Family Experiences Result in Higher Levels of Kindness and Flexibility
There are a number of considerations to take into account regarding the family background of a potential future spouse:

- How did his or her family express anger? How did they express love?

- How was responsibility handled?

- Was the family environment permissive or authoritarian?

- Was an appropriate amount of attention given to children, or were they spoiled or perhaps neglected?

- How were possessions handled?

A positive experience in the family of one's childhood usually results in emotional maturity as well as higher levels of flexibility and kindness. Family background is an important component in predicting couples' overall relationship quality, unless tremendous efforts are made by the couple to overcome these shortcomings.

An Example Illustrating How Family Background Influences Our Expectations: Sita devi dasi (not her real name) was raised in Eastern Europe, the youngest of six children. Her father handled all the finances and made most of the decisions in the family. Her mother loved her domestic responsibilities and felt protected. Her parents argued occasionally, but her father quickly made the final decision. Dhruva dasa (not his real name) was born in the United States. His parents divorced when he was young, and his mother took all the responsibility for raising him and his brother. Sita was impressed by Dhruva's understanding of devotional service and saw him as a protective authority figure similar to her own father. Dhruva, however, after seeing how hard it was for his mother to do everything alone, didn't want to take up the sole role of authority in the relationship. He was looking for more of an egalitarian friendship. Also, Sita wanted a large family and thought Dhruva would gradually change his mind about wanting only one or two children.

Dhruva began to feel that Sita was seeing him through her expectations, not as he really was. They had been associating for a few months and were under some pressure from the elders in their community to get married. When he realized the extent of their different expectations, Dhruva decided not to continue with the relationship. The point here is that the traits and patterns which you see in the family background of your potential spouse are most likely the traits and patterns that they will bring to your marriage. This is especially important once you start rearing a family.

Compatibility

Be Wary of Extreme Differences – When trying to determine compatibility, it is important to understand that some differences will always be there. Some variety does indeed add spice to life, but be wary of extreme differences. How do you know if those differences will harm your relationship or enhance it? Dr. John Van Epp (*How to Avoid Falling in Love with a Jerk,* McGraw Hill, 2008) suggests the following:

- Acknowledge the differences

- Next, determine if the differences are mutually beneficial (Are you a better person with your partner than you would be without him or her?)

- Finally, there must be a deep and mutual appreciation of the differences

A person who is very introverted may at first appreciate the outgoing nature of a socialite who can't stand to miss any get-together. However, over time the introvert may find that particular characteristic irritating. On the other hand, a person who is just a little shy may be able to develop more social skills in the company of a partner who is a bit more confident and comfortable in social situations. The idea is to avoid extreme differences that will ultimately lead to conflict.

Similar Commitment to the Ideals of Krishna Consciousness – An essential aspect of compatibility for a devotee couple is that both partners have a similar interest in and commitment to the ideals of Krishna consciousness as demonstrated through their spiritual practices. In addition, it is helpful if both devotees' philosophical orientation toward the teachings of Lord Chaitanya in Gaudiya Vaishnavism can easily be harmonized.

A neophyte in devotional service may naively think that all that is needed for a good marriage is to marry a devotee, and that the necessity of compatible natures is just a "material consideration." While time has shown that compatibility

> The phrase 'like disposition' is very significant. Formerly, boys and girls of similar dispositions were married; the similar natures of the boy and girl were united in order to make them happy.
>
> *Srimad-Bhagavatam* 3.21.15, purport

with a marriage partner makes life so much easier, one should never minimize how much mutual spiritual practice is essential. Sharing our sadhana, devotional aspirations, and service can be tremendously strengthening.

Compatibility in Personality, Values, and Lifestyle – The important areas to consider for compatibility are personality, values, and lifestyle.[4] The more two personalities are similar, the more likely it is that they will be compatible over time.

As a couple, examine your basic emotional temperaments and consider the ways in which you are different.

Take a look at how each of you manages your finances. Is one a big spender and the other thrifty? Discover the other person's attitudes toward "things." How do they handle financial stress? As Dr. John Van Epp[5] says, "Much can be learned about a prospective partner by recognizing how that person handles their money and their possessions. If you entrusted your finances into the hands of your partner, how similarly or differently would he or she do things? Would your needs and interests be considered?"

Honestly decide if you can really be comfortable with your differences.

Numerous surveys concur that above all else, most people simply want a deep relationship of friendship with their marriage partner. The more interests and activities that you enjoy in common, the more likely it is that you will enjoy loving feelings, security, and satisfaction in your relationship.

Arranged Marriages – Traditionally, similar areas of compatibility were used as criteria for arranged marriages. Elders would first of all make sure that the two parties were from respectable families of similar status. They would then examine the horoscopes to see if the couple had compatible natures. Finally, they would research the prospective spouse's character and his or her reputation for dealing with others. Was a person financially and behaviorally responsible?

These same criteria should be used today, either by elders, or by yourself if you are choosing alone. Careful thought and research on the idea of compatibility should not be minimized on so important a life choice as marriage.

Astrology is sometimes recommended to help ascertain compatibility. If you have the means and know an expert astrologer, the astrologer may be able to check possible outcomes of your intertwining karmas.

> Not more than twenty-five years ago, and perhaps it is still current, parents in India used to consult the horoscope of the boy and girl to see whether there would be factual union in their psychological conditions. These considerations are very important.
>
> *Srimad-Bhagavatam* 3.21.15, purport

Arranged Marriages Versus Marriages Based on Initial Attraction – Speaking of arranged marriages, a study by Dr. Robert Epstein published in the January/February 2010 issue of "Scientific American Mind" had some interesting observations. Among other things, it noted that in most countries marriage relationships are entered into based on bodily attraction and feelings of love. Unfortunately, those feelings decreased rapidly within 18 months. In many arranged marriages of India, he discovered that although feelings of love were not a component in the beginning of an arranged marriage, those feelings quickly grew. It is understood that if compatible persons are matched, love can develop. He observed that after 10 years of arranged marriage, the feelings of love were often twice as strong as in the types of marriage that had been based on initial "chemistry." **This demonstrates that love can develop from mutual service.** Couples in arranged marriages have strong commitment, and they make the effort to work things out.

It is usually best to allow plenty of time for getting to know a potential spouse. Many patterns of a person's emotional temperament will not emerge until a pattern has gone full cycle. It can take up to three months for a pattern to emerge, and it can take up to two years for you to know a person well enough to be reasonably sure of your compatibility.

Caution: Red Flag Warnings

Certain behavior patterns serve as warnings for potential relationship problems. Be cautious in the presence of these red flags; they could indicate trouble somewhere in the future. The following are behavior patterns of concern:

- **Poor treatment of others** is one such red flag. There is a real correlation between how we treat others and how we will treat our spouses after marriage. After the euphoria of your new marriage has worn off, your spouse's poor treatment of others will soon become poor treatment of you. Avoid people who are fundamentally unkind.

- **Incongruence (inconsistency) between actions and words.** If a person exhibits attitudes and behaviors in the present that are not typical of their attitudes and behaviors in the past, chances are that what you see now are not their real attitudes.

- **Unhealthy ways of meeting emotional needs.** Survival strategies from a difficult childhood can be ingrained and very counterproductive.

- **Inability to empathize with another's feelings.** This is a very large red flag.

- **Blaming you or others.** Another very large red flag to avoid is a 'blamer.' If you don't want to end up in a relationship where you often feel resentment or feel like you are walking on thin ice – avoid blamers. The "Law of Blame"[6] is that it eventually goes to the closest person. When you become the closest person, the blame will eventually fall on you.

- **Thinking You Can "Change" the Other Person.** Seeing a red flag and thinking that "you will change them" is in itself a very big red flag.

You cannot anticipate every problem but you do want to be cautious and watch for undesirable personality traits.

Safe people are those who give their word and then stick to it. They don't spring unpleasant surprises on you. They don't take you for granted. They follow through with what they say they will do, or try to make up for it if they cannot. They apologize for lapses and inform you in advance of changes.

Unsafe people are inconsistent, do not keep their word, often claim they "forgot," take you for granted, break boundaries with no thought or care, cannot empathize with your pain or disappointments, and leave you to fend for yourself once they are done with you. It is difficult to trust such people, and even more difficult to have long and happy marriage relationships with them. Their history can often reveal numerous broken relationships.

Associate in a Variety of Circumstances – You will never get to know another person unless time is set aside for mutual disclosure and a variety of experiences together. Here is a situation that shows the importance of this: Sundari (not her real name) approached a friend of mine, asking if my friend could give her some guidelines to determine if the man she was associating with, Shastra (not his real name), was a good choice for her. My friend recommended that they try to associate in a variety of circumstances. Sundari and Shastra were both Temple devotees at the time, and Shastra was known to Sundari as a scholarly book distributor. So far, they had just been conversing in between performing their service at the Temple.

After receiving my friend's advice, Sundari decided to travel a short distance by train with Shastra to visit his mother. As they were trying to get off the train, the door jammed and he got so angry that he smashed the window on the door. Thus Sundari saw a side of Shastra that otherwise she might not have seen till after they were married.

Upon her return, Sundari profusely thanked my friend for suggesting that she associate with Shastra in a variety of circumstances. How your partner acts in various circumstances is far more telling than how he or she treats you during the courtship phase of your relationship.

Phone or Internet Conversations Are Not Enough – Just conversing together (for example, by internet or phone) may not be a complete indication of compatibility, and doing many things together but not engaging in continually deeper levels of mutual self disclosure may also not be sufficient. You need both to examine your full range of compatibility. It is advisable that you work on any things that need changing in the relationship before you marry. An ounce of pre-marital insight is worth a pound of post–marital problem solving.

May We Have Your Blessings?

Our Parents and Friends May See Things We Cannot – We all need blessings; the more we get the better off we are. Seek the blessings of your *shiksha* (instructing) and *diksha* (initiating) gurus, relatives, and other elders in your community. How will you feel about your upcoming marriage if you don't have the support of your parents, friends, and others that matter to you? Take the time to really listen to them and see if they have any reservations about your decision. They may see things that you cannot. Thank them for their concern and give yourself some time to think about what they might have said. Ask others who are close to you if they feel the same way. It may be that others' concerns are not within your value system, and that their opinions truly do not matter to you; the idea is to be as introspective as possible. After all, it's possible that the concerns expressed by a friend or relative today could become your problems later in life.

Consider Values, Cultural Background, and Religious Background – Make sure you know your values. In the case of marrying someone from a different cultural background, your values may seem similar in your present situation but may eventually emerge to be quite different as you begin to raise children and pursue your careers. Inter-cultural as well as inter-religious marriages are some of the hardest to negotiate. Remember that in the areas of personality, values, lifestyle, and family background, it is best to have as many similarities as possible.

Depending on Krishna and the Power of Prayer – Marriage is an important samskara, a sacred rite of passage, in your life. Your decision will govern much of the course of the rest of your life. Not only do you need to pray for a good life partner, but you need to continually pray throughout your marriage for yourself, your spouse, and your family. All relationships need continual adjustment as people and situations change.

> Only by God's grace can one get a nice wife just as he desires. Similarly, it is only by God's grace that a girl gets a husband suitable to her heart. Thus it is said that if we pray to the Supreme Lord in every transaction of our material existence, everything will be done very nicely and just suitable to our heart's desire. In other words in all circumstances we must take shelter of the Supreme Personality of Godhead and depend completely on His decision.
>
> [*Srimad-Bhagavatam* 3.21.28, purport]

Conclusion

Living Happily Ever After – Even though there are many profound joys in married life, I would like to suggest a small change to the fairytale ending of living "happily ever after." It would be more accurate to say that after the marriage ceremony, you then begin the "hard work of living happily ever after."

In the published study referred to earlier, Dr. Epstein identified the essential factors which caused increased feelings of love within marriage. Foremost among these were commitment and communication. Also included in that list were sharing secrets, accommodation (altering one's behavior to meet the needs of another), and seeing one's spouse in a vulnerable state. Dr. Epstein emphasized the need for the ongoing practice of building your marital skills. With good mentoring and training, positive actions can be learned.

Importance of Practicing Relationship Skills – My husband and I share many interests and have always enjoyed practicing our sadhana together. In our beginning days in Krishna consciousness, we performed Deity worship together and could often be seen going for a walk together in the afternoons, while the Deities were resting, my husband holding a volume of *Srimad-Bhagavatam* and reading out loud to me as we walked. Over the years, we read through the complete series several times. As our children grew, our services evolved, and we struggled to support our growing family. We gradually experienced less connection along with some signs of tension between us. However, since we began learning, teaching, and practicing a variety of relationship skills, our relationship dramatically deepened. We experience the benefit of ongoing practice in building our own marital skills.

Importance of Premarital Education – Premarital education is highly recommended before marriage as well as attending skill building courses periodically throughout marriage. In temples in Canada, we do not perform wedding ceremonies for devotees until they undergo some premarital education. We want to support their ongoing relationship and spiritual wellbeing, not just simply perform ceremonies. In addition, the Grihastha Vision Team trains happy, long-term married couples to mentor new couples. We also facilitate grihastha workshops for ongoing marital success.

Commitment and Dedication to the Marriage Itself – If there is one final word regarding a happy and lasting marriage, it would be the principle of commitment and dedication while sharing a spiritual purpose. In the most successful marriages, both partners are more committed to the health and longevity of the marriage than to their often changing feelings toward each other. That way, during those times when two individuals who made vows of lasting commitment can't stand each other – and those times will surely come, since no one is perfect – they have something to fall back on and remain committed to. Couples must learn the fine art of working out their differences and praying to Krishna for help. Differences, when negotiated compassionately, grow into stronger bonds of love.

Building a happy marriage is a service to yourselves, your families, and the future of the movement. Good marriages will enable us to live up to the appellation of being "Happy Krishnas."

About the Author

UTTAMA DEVI DASI was initiated by Srila Prabhupada in 1973, along with her husband Partha dasa. They have three children and five grandchildren. She has performed a variety of services through the years – *pujari* work, head Deity seamstress, teaching, and management. She has taken relationship education training from Prepare and Enrich Canada©, Dasi Ziyad Family Institute, and Compassion Power©. She really enjoys working with youth, teaching them the *Bhagavad-gita* and relationship skills. Her present passion is traveling with her husband and facilitating grihastha workshops. (Give them a call!) At present they live in their forest home in Saranagati Village in British Columbia, Canada, where they do premarital education for devotees via Skype, while eating home grown veggies.

Chapter 3 Let's Talk About It: Open and Honest Communication

Mantrini devi dasi

In this chapter you will learn:

✓ Ways We Communicate

✓ What Undermines Good Communication

✓ Healthy vs. Unhealthy Communication

✓ Empathic Listening Statements, the SOLER Formula, and "I" Messages

✓ The Speaker-Listener Technique and the "X-Y-Z Statement"

✓ The Difference Between "Intent" and "Impact" in Communication

✓ Filters that Block Good Communication and How to Deal with Them

✓ Relevance to Spiritual Relationships

Half Baked
© David Musterer

"I know that you believe you understand what you think I said, but I'm not sure you realize what you heard is not what I meant."

Principles Highlighted in this Chapter

- Open and Honest Communication
- Mutual Respect and Appreciation

What is Open and Honest Communication?

It has been said that two monologues do not make a dialogue. How many of our conversations between devotees, especially in married life, fall into this category? Aren't we really longing for heart to heart communication with our spouse and children?

Revealing one's heart and mind in confidence and listening confidentially to others is an important exchange between Vaishnavas. Verse Four of the *Nectar of Instruction* states:

> Offering gifts in charity, accepting charitable gifts, revealing one's mind in confidence, inquiring confidentially, accepting *prasada* and offering *prasada* are the six symptoms of love shared by one devotee and another.

Open and honest communication is a key principle behind a Krishna conscious family life. It is the basis of healthy relationships that endure. However, unless we had parents who modeled healthy communication patterns, we need to take some time to learn these skills. Not only will this contribute to making our family life happy and blessed, but if we master them, we will be teaching our children valuable skills for use in their future relationships.

Looking at my own marriage (we have been together now over 43 years), I see it as an example of how the power of learning and using better communication skills can improve marriage quality and the quality of all family interactions. Neither my husband nor I grew up in a family that used functional communication. My family was characterized by a lot of shouting and uncontrolled emotions, with lots of conflicts that never got resolved. My husband's family was just the opposite – no one talked about their feelings, conflicts were hushed up, and only superficial topics were discussed. Imagine what it was like for us when we got married! My husband thought that if I raised my voice, we were on the verge of a divorce! On the other hand, he could go to bed in the middle of an argument and instantly fall asleep while I lay there fuming!

Over the years, we were introduced to counseling principles which included the study of dysfunctional families, which led to further study of topics such as conflict resolution and communication skills. Little by little we began incorporating some of these skills into our marriage and family. I still remember our ten year old daughter announcing that she did not want us to use those "methods" on her! She was referring to empathic listening statements beginning with "You feel…" She had read one of the books on effective parenting we had lying around, and she was "on to us" with our new ways of communicating! She was keenly aware that these techniques did not come naturally to us. Our younger daughter, however, loved it when we used empathic listening! She was a more emotional child and loved feeling validated.

It took many years, but my husband and I were able to bridge the gap between my "enmeshed" family system (characterized by frequent crossing of emotional boundaries) and my husband's "disengaged" family system (with few emotional connections). Eventually our success was so apparent that we became encouraged to create ways to apply our knowledge to help others. We began to study both marriage counseling and individual counseling in earnest, in the hopes of helping other couples. Not only has our marriage benefitted, but our children have had better family communication modeling. In turn, their marriages will be easier and happier.

Now, let us take a look at the following material which contains methods to help us improve our ability to communicate – to speak and listen effectively from the heart. They are building blocks for marriages and all healthy relationships. There are many good references, books and seminars which teach these principles. I have included only the highlights to pique your interest in further study. Let's begin at the beginning…what IS communication?

The Four Ways We Communicate

Without much thought, we naturally use these four ways to communicate.

1.	Actions	"What we do"
2.	Words	"What we say"
3.	Tone of Voice	"How we say it"
4.	Appearance	Expressions, body language, dress

But, what messages are we sending? Do we send mixed messages – do our words match our actions? Do we blame or criticize others because of our own emotional states? Do we half listen to others, while constructing in our heads a snappy "come-back"? Most likely, we do not think too much about it one way or another, and it is not surprising that we may be frustrated when we do not get the results we want. However, with skills training we can learn to improve our communication to reach the level of good or healthy communication, an essential building block for happy and peaceful grihastha life.

What exactly is good or healthy communication? Good communication patterns are learned skills and take some time to master. We can understand it better by taking a look at "what it is not." The following section outlines actions that undermine or go against good communication.

DID YOU KNOW? One study showed that 55% of the emotional meaning of what you say is expressed by your facial expression. Only 7% of the emotional meaning is verbal.

How to Undermine Communication

The following is a list of communication patterns that are regularly used by all of us – but, unfortunately, they often have an undesirable effect. They "undermine" good communication because they trigger the other person to either become defensive or withdraw. Even if some of the actions may look on the surface as "positive" (such as approving or advising), they ultimately undermine communication because the other person is more likely to try to "please or placate" you than communicate how they are really thinking or feeling. Take a look at the following chart to see how many you can recognize as part of your communication style.

Instructing	"You should…" or "You have to…"
Threatening	"If you do this, what will happen is…" or "You better do what I'm telling you or else…"
Referring to Oneself (Autobiography)	"When I was a brahmachari, we were much more austere."
Advising	"You better drop your studies" or "The best thing you can do is…"
Preaching	"Men don't cry." or "This is what Prabhupada wanted us to do."
Interpreting	"What you actually want is to attract their attention." or "That means you're committing offences…"
Evaluating	"That's awful!" or "There's nothing to worry about!"
Approving	"You're completely right…" or "Yes, that's exactly what's going on."
Disapproving	"No, that's not true." or "What you're saying is just ridiculous."
Criticizing, insulting	"This has happened to you because you're stupid."
Ridiculing	"Yeah, right, leave your husband, leave your work and move in the Temple – you're such a pure devotee!"
Questioning, Probing	"When? Where? Why?" or "What was your relationship with your mother?"

Communication Blocks Between Spouses

From the chart above, we have seen how some communication patterns undermine the process of healthy communication. Now, let's take a look at communication blocks that commonly happen between spouses. We have also provided possible solutions you can put to work immediately:

1. **Rolling your eyes while your spouse is talking.** *Solution*: Try to understand the true meaning behind your spouse's words. Is there an angle or an aspect of your spouse's position with which you can agree?

2. **Responding with "Do we have to talk about that again?"** *Solution*: Don't avoid conflict…It's always better to resolve issues early before they grow in size. It's like pulling weeds in your garden. Weeding early and often keeps your "relationship garden" in good shape.

3. **Yawning and looking bored.** *Solution*: Showing respect for your spouse is always the best course of action, and it models the behavior you would like in return.

4. **Repeatedly looking at your watch**. *Solution*: Remember, your goal is to continuously build goodwill with your partner. One way to do that is to invest time in the relationship.

5. **Continuing to work on the computer or read a book.** *Solution*: Schedule time to talk with your spouse when there are no distractions. Isn't it all about prioritizing the important things in life and consciously deciding that your grihastha life is worth the effort?

6. **Replying "Nothing" when asked what's on your mind.** *Solution*: Meaningful talk requires honesty and vulnerability, which in turn requires courage. Meaningful talk is the only way to create deep emotional and spiritual connection.

7. **Refusing to interact when your spouse is trying to talk to you.** *Solution*: Marital success requires humility and respect. These qualities are more powerful than any amount of holding back from your partner.

8. **Changing the subject abruptly.** *Solution*: Practicing good manners with your spouse goes a long way in maintaining harmony in grihastha life. Try to respect your spouse – a Vaishnava loved by Lord Krishna – even when you disagree.

9. **Turning and walking away while your spouse is talking**. *Solution*: Sometimes walking away can be a defense reaction. It is based on fear – fear of confrontation, fear of rejection, or fear of anger. Instead, face your fear. That is the definition of courage.

10. **Coming up with perpetual excuses to postpone the conversation.** *Solution*: Think of the big picture. What kind of marriage do you want, and how are you going to achieve it? Be honest with yourself and take responsibility for your part of creating an ideal grihastha relationship.

Adapted from Nancy J. Wasson, PhD, co-author of
Keep Your Marriage[1]

Healthy Communication

We hear a lot about "healthy communication." What exactly is the essence of good communication between grihasthas? It is said that "long after people forget what you did and said, they will remember how you made them feel."

> **TIP**: Don't assume your spouse is a mind reader: After spending a long time with someone, we assume that they know what we meant or how we are feeling. However, this is not the case. Very often when there is a miscommunication and a flare up, this assumption is at fault.

So, a good definition of healthy communication between devotees includes how the participants feel during and after the experience. It is safe to say, then, that healthy communication occurs when two people are able to express their needs, wants, and feelings clearly, specifically, and authentically, and have these expressions received with *care*, *respect*, and *attention*. This care, respect, and attention is basic Vaishnava etiquette; it is easy to forget that our partners are Vaishnavas first and foremost.

Why Learn Communication Skills?

If we have never taken the time to learn good communication skills, we may minimize their importance. Or maybe, having heard that in business or at work we need to use good communication skills to sell a product or promote the business, we may think that's only for the business world. With our loved ones, we may think that we can just "be ourselves." Our family members should automatically know that no matter how we speak to them, we basically love them and accept them. Is this really true? Not according to the research done by Dr. John Gottman,[2] author of *The Seven Principles for Making a Marriage Work*. Dr. John Gottman can predict with 96% accuracy within the first three minutes of a couple having a conversation whether the relationship he is watching will survive over the

> **TIP**: Although not always true for everyone, men and women generally communicate differently. Being aware of this can enhance your listening skills. Men often talk because they want to give information or solve a problem. Women tend to talk to connect with someone or to get information. Women usually talk more about relationships than men. Men are often more concerned about details than women.

long-haul or not. He bases his predictions on four potentially destructive communication styles and coping mechanisms.

So, if destructive communication styles can destroy a marriage, isn't it worth our while to take some time to learn healthy communication skills? Let's begin with some simple listening rules called "attending behaviors" – also known as the "**SOLER**" formula, developed by Gerard Egan.[3]

The "SOLER" Formula – Using Body Language to Further Good Communication

The **"SOLER"** formula is an easy way to remember some important body language techniques. These are simple ways to best position our bodies and attention to maximize our communication potential:

> **S – Sitting Posture Facing Squarely** This indicates you are ready and available to hear the speaker.
>
> **O – Open Body Language** Do not cross arms or legs; rather rest arms on lap and place both feet on the floor in a relaxed manner. This shows openness and non-defensiveness.
>
> **L – Listening Attentively by Leaning toward the Speaker** "Leaning in" towards the speaker shows attentiveness and interest.
>
> **E – Eye Contact** Avoid staring, but show interest by looking at the face of the speaker. Avoid looking around the room, at a computer screen, newspaper, etc.
>
> **R – Remain Relaxed** This demonstrates confidence and helps the other person relax.

At first, it may seem artificial to try to remember to do these things, but with practice, it will become second-nature.

Empathic Listening Statements – Hearing with Your Heart

Empathic Listening Statements – Now that we know some "attending behaviors," it is time to learn how to use some "active" or "empathic" listening statements. Empathic listening is a combination of communication skills and the desire to genuinely connect with your partner. It is frequently referred to as "hearing with your heart." Often, the result is that your partner will feel more willing to talk about what is really bothering him or her, and thus you both achieve a deeper sense of connection.

Have you ever really been excited about something, then felt disappointed with the response you got? Maybe you said,

"Guess what! I just paid off my credit card!"

And your friend might retort,

"Big deal…you will probably just get in debt again!"

How does that feel?

Or he might think he is encouraging you, but actually is diverting the attention towards himself by saying,

"Congratulations. I did that two years ago."

We would feel much more supported if he had said,

"Wow! It must be a great relief to be out of debt."

You might then feel like saying even more about what a debt burden you were experiencing, which might lead to a deeper level of communication.

The following chart shows some empathic listening categories, their description and examples of the kinds of things to say.

Empathic Listening Categories		
Action	**Description**	**Examples**
Encourage	Don't agree or disagree; use neutral words.	"Tell me more…"
Clarify	Ask questions; restate wrong interpretations to make the speaker explain further.	"How long ago did this happen?"
Restate	Restate the basic ideas and facts.	"So you would like your friend to be more dependable?"
Reflect	Reflect the speaker's basic feelings.	"You're really upset."
Summarize	Restate the most important ideas including feelings.	"You've expressed these main points…"
Validate	Acknowledge the value of their concerns and feelings; appreciate their efforts and actions.	"I appreciate how you want to get this straightened out."

This type of listening takes some practice. Don't be too hard on yourself if you don't get the hang of it right away. If you are not sure which type of empathic listening category to use, try to guess the unexpressed need by asking yourself, "What is my partner wanting? What does my partner need?" Then, you can try one of the following lead-ins:

1. Seems as if you wish...?

2. Were you wanting...?

3. Are you hoping...?

Empathic listening is a skill important enough to take some extra time to master. Your local library will have a variety of books on the subject, which will help you understand the basic principles. Also, marriage education trainings such as PREP© (Preparation and Relationship Enhancement Program)[4] offer workshops where you can get "hands-on" practice in communication skills.

Concrete Speaking Skills – Speaking with Clarity and Purpose

Now that we have become aware of some listening and attending skills, let's take a look at speaking skills. Do we make clear statements about what we want, think or feel? Or are we vague, expecting our spouse to be able to "know" or "mind-read" what we are trying to communicate? First of all, let's look at concrete speaking skills and the difference between thoughts and feelings. To be able to speak with clarity, we need to know the difference between an experience, a behavior, and a feeling.

> **An experience** is something that happens to you. *Example:* "My alarm didn't go off this morning so I didn't make it to *mangala arati* for early morning worship."

> **A behavior** is something you do (or fail to do). *Example:* "I usually get up at 4:00 a.m."

> **A feeling** is the emotion associated with the experience or behavior. *Example:* "I feel guilty when I sleep late and miss the morning program."

Most of us don't have a problem understanding the difference between an experience and a behavior. However, we often confuse thoughts and feelings. An example of this would be to say, "I *feel* that you are making a mistake." Although the statement uses the word "feel," what is actually being expressed is a "thought." So, it is more accurate to say, "I *think* that you are making a mistake."

"Feeling" Word List

The following is a list of "feeling" words, expressions of emotions. We will need "feeling" words later when we learn a skill called the "X-Y-Z Statement." This list is by no means complete, but it gives you the general idea.

Positive Feelings:

enchanted	infatuated	tender	smart
vibrant	independent	capable	comfortable
happy	proud	gratified	daring
worthy	sympathetic	important	warm
concerned	appreciated	consoled	untroubled
delighted	eager	optimistic	sure
joyful	hopeful	valiant	amazed
brave	brilliant	liked	content
cared for	affectionate	fond	comfortable
excited	patient	strong	relaxed
inspired	amused	yearning	at ease
popular	peaceful	determined	wide awake
pleased	excited	jolly	benevolent
relieved	glad	adventurous	friendly
peaceful	intelligent		

Negative Feelings:

troubled	disdainful	contemptuous	alarmed
annoyed	disgusted	resentful	fed-up
frustrated	depressed	dissatisfied	fatigued
useless	weak	hopeless	forlorn
rejected	guilty	embarrassed	inhibited
bewildered	frightened	dismayed	disturbed
antagonistic	vengeful	indignant	mad
torn	unloved	angry	hurt
miserable	in pain	lonely	worthless
futile	abandoned	estranged	degraded
humiliated	shocked	panicky	horrified

Using "I" messages

Using "I" messages does two things: it helps us communicate with others, and it keeps us from feeling like a victim. "I" messages break down barriers, allowing us to listen to each other. "You" messages put up walls because we are busy defending ourselves from attack. An "I" message is constructed as follows: "I feel *(feeling)* when *(this happens)* because *(why)*." Look at the two examples below. See the difference in the "I" message and the "You" message:

"I" Message:	"You" Message:
"I feel worried when you don't tell me where you are and when you are coming home because I am afraid of what might have happened. I'm afraid that you might be lying in the middle of the street somewhere…"	"Why didn't you call? You make me so mad when you don't call. How many times do I have to tell you to call me? You could be dead in some alley somewhere, and I wouldn't know about it…"

Both are saying essentially the same thing, but the first is easier to listen to. Before you make an "I" statement, ask yourself the following questions:

- *What am I feeling?*
- *When am I feeling it?*
- *Why am I feeling it?*

Use "feeling" words such as "uncomfortable", "hurt", "angry", or "worried". Being specific helps the listener to understand exactly what you are upset about and why. If you are not specific enough, it is easier for the other person to deny that it happened or to question what you are talking about.

Avoid "you" statements such as "I feel that you…," or "You make me feel…," or "You are so…"

X-Y-Z Statements

> **TIP**: Learning to use "I" messages can be like learning a foreign language. In foreign languages the grammar is different so you need to learn different sentence structures. As a result you are going to be stumbling over sentences for a while. Practice helps.

Part of speaking with clarity is communicating our thoughts, wants, and feelings briefly and concisely. The more we are clear about these things, the better our spouse can understand what we thinking, wanting, and feeling. Misunderstandings come about when we are vague or think our spouse should intuitively "know" or "mind-read" our desires. The PREP© model teaches the following skill that assists us speaking with clarity and brevity.

The "X-Y-Z Statement" Formula: The formula consists of making the three statements on the next page in 1-2-3 order, filling in the blanks to fit your situation.

Step One: "When you do **X** _____" (example: *"stay out late at night," "don't look for a job," "let the laundry pile up,"* etc.) State a *specific behavior*, not a character flaw! Behavior can change. Do not expect a change in personality.

Step Two: "In situation **Y** _____" (example: *"and I am home alone," "when we have no income," "and I am counting on clean clothes,"* etc.) State a *specific setting*. Limit it to a specific problem, not everything that is wrong in the relationship.

Step Three: "I feel **Z** _____" (example: *"lonely, abandoned," "anxious, concerned, fearful," "uncared for, ignored, slighted,"* etc.) Communicate a *specific feeling*, not a thought. (Go back to the list of "feeling" words if you need help...or see the chart below for a quick refresher.)

Feelings	Thoughts
I feel lonely, sad, bored	you are mean, inconsiderate
I feel afraid, scared, worried	you are not Krishna conscious
I feel abandoned, anxious, rejected	you are stupid, spaced out

This model clearly states the behavior that concerns you, limits it to a specific circumstance, and describes how it impacts you, the speaker. Our goals of brevity and clarity are easily met. Also, as an added benefit, expressing how things affect you can be a *powerful motivator* for change in the other person or the relationship! We aren't always aware of how our behavior impacts our spouse. To hear a clear statement like an x-y-z Statement AND to hear how the other person feels as a result is very powerful stuff!

An added point: to be most effective when sharing your feelings, go for the most honest emotion. Going beyond your reluctance to seem emotionally vulnerable can bring huge rewards towards deepening your marital relationship!

> TIP: Anger is a "secondary" emotion. It covers up deeper, more vulnerable emotions. Most people don't react positively to someone else's anger. It makes them defensive. We DO respond, however, to more vulnerable emotions, especially when they are expressed by a loved one.

Speaker-Listener Technique

Empathic listening, which is listening from the heart, and concrete speaking, which is speaking with clarity and purpose, are necessary tools, but they will not be sufficient to deal with the inevitable power struggle or conflict that comes about in long-term, intimate relationships such as marriage. Power struggles involve having to be "right" or win the argument or have the last word. Here are some more skills we can use to tackle such harder communication challenges.

The following model as taught by PREP INC. combines speaking and listening in a unique way – and is aptly called the "speaker-listener" technique. The "speaker-listener" technique is a deliberate and structured process of discussing topics that have been sources of conflict in the past. It not only helps couples work through long-standing conflict, but it often uncovers "hidden issues" in the relationship, which is a first step in dealing with them.

How It Works

Speaker-Listener technique is used when a couple is having a problem or conflict. There are rules for the speaker and rules for the listener. In a nutshell, each spouse gets a turn at speaking, while the other spouse listens and paraphrases. Then they switch speaking and listening roles. They keep switching between being the speaker and being the listener until the problem or conflict is resolved. Often, new clarity is achieved, or perhaps a hidden issue arises. Take a look at the rules for each:

Rules for Speaker:

- Speak for yourself – use "I" messages (*"I think..." "I want..." "I feel..."*)

- Don't go on and on. (It's better to be heard thoroughly on one point than to make four points and have your spouse miss most of them...)

- Stop after each point and let your spouse paraphrase what you said.

- If the paraphrase isn't correct, restate the part they didn't get.

- When the listener gets the paraphrase right, it's their turn to speak.

Rules for Listener:

- Focus on what the speaker is saying. (Don't be thinking of a rebuttal. You will have to be able to paraphrase correctly what your spouse said and that will be enough work.)

- Paraphrase what you heard. (*"I'm hearing that..."* or *"I'm understanding that..."*)

- At the end of the paraphrase, clarify by asking, *"Did I get that right?"*

- If you didn't get it exactly right, don't give up, keep trying until you do.

Rules for Both:

- The speaker has the floor! Do not interrupt while the speaker is speaking. You will have your turn.

- Speaker keeps the floor until the listener paraphrases correctly.

- Share the floor...don't monopolize the conversation.

In the beginning stages of learning this Speaker-Listener technique, some props are sometimes helpful. In the PREP system, a piece of floor tile is held by the speaker – indicating that that person has the "floor." Other systems use a picture of a microphone that the speaker holds. In any case, the prop helps us by giving the speaker permission to speak without interruption and reminds the listener not to interrupt. At first, the "rules" for the technique seem to make the conversation feel "artificial," but with practice, it becomes more natural.

Hidden Issues

> **TIP**: Many couples find that if they agree to set aside a time each day (or once a week) to use this technique – a "speaker-listener" time – they are more likely to actually do it.

The Speaker-Listener technique is so effective in processing conflicts that hidden issues naturally come up. Hidden issues are core reasons for conflicts that are not apparent when couples are locked in a power struggle over a problem.

Most core reasons for conflict in marriage involve the need for acceptance. Take a look at the following list of ways married couples want acceptance:

- We want to be cared for (acceptance of our needs)
- We want to be esteemed (acceptance of how lovable we are)
- We want to be respected (acceptance of how valuable we are)
- We want to be listened to (acceptance of the value of our opinions)
- We want to be empowered (acceptance of our influence)
- We want to be appreciated (acceptance of our uniqueness)

By using the Speaker-Listener technique, power struggles are short-circuited by the listening and speaking rules, which demonstrate respect for, interest in, and appreciation for the other spouse.

> **NOTE:** When dealing with hidden issues, the Speaker-Listener technique focuses less on problem solving and more on hearing each other's thoughts and feelings. The most powerful form of acceptance is really listening to the thoughts and feelings of your mate. You may not be able to "fix" deeply hidden issues with one discussion, but you will engender more love and trust. This will lead to a willingness to explore the issue further at another time.

Communication Skills in Action

Let's take a look at a common scenario in families: getting the family ready to start the day. First, we will look at an exchange between a couple who let a critical remark start a conflict, which quickly escalates into all out war! Then, we will replay the scenario using some of the communication skills we have been talking about, so you can see the difference. Here is the scenario without using the skills:

> **She:** Here's your toast, dear…
>
> **He:** It looks a little burnt!
>
> **She:** It's not burned! It's just a little brown!
>
> **He:** Charred to a crisp is what I would say!
>
> **She:** Well, what do you expect when I'm slaving away getting breakfast for everyone, packing lunches, and YOU sit there and complain about your toast!
>
> **He:** I think you're just disorganized! I mean, just look at the mess in this house! You're home all day. Why can't you get it together?!
>
> **She:** Well, you don't ever do anything to help me, even when you are here!
>
> **He:** That's a laugh! I go to work every day so you'll have money!
>
> **She:** You aren't exactly bringing in the big bucks!
>
> **He:** Well, that's a real materialistic thing to say!
>
> **She:** Materialistic! What about you and your GIANT HD TV!!!

Here is the same situation, except the wife expresses her feelings in an X-Y-Z Statement, giving the husband an opportunity to use empathic listening. See the difference in the ending:

> **She:** Here's your toast, dear…
>
> **He:** It looks a little burnt!
>
> **She:** It's not burned! It's just a little brown!
>
> **He:** Charred to a crisp is what I would say!
>
> **She:** Well, what do you expect when I'm slaving away getting breakfast for everyone, packing lunches, and YOU sit there and complain about your toast!

He: I think you're just disorganized! I mean, just look at the mess in this house! You're home all day. Why can't you get it together?!

She: When you criticize me while I am working so hard to keep the family together, it makes me feel unappreciated. *(X-Y-Z Statement "When you do __X__ in this situation ____Y____, it makes me feel _____Z_____.)*

He: You feel that I don't appreciate you…Is that right? *(empathic listening)*

She: Well, yes, especially about the contribution I make to the family…

He: While I do appreciate what you do, sometimes I wish things could be more organized around the house. *("I" message)*

She: I understand that you want things to be more organized. Is that right? *(empathic listening)*

He: Yes, I do wish things went more smoothly at home.

She: We're in a rush now. Let's find some time to talk about how we could share the household responsibilities.

He: Good plan. How about tonight after the kids are in bed?

The second scenario shows how a few minutes devoted to talking about how certain actions impact our feelings and then responding with empathic listening can change the whole tenor of the conflict. Instead of all out war, complete with accusations and hurt feelings, this couple was able to make a plan to solve the problem.

> **TIP:** When a conversation starts to escalate into conflict or worse, switch to an X-Y-Z statement (see the section of X-Y-Z statements) and be ready to use empathic listening. The whole mood will change for the better, and you will be in a better position to solve the conflict.

Intent and Impact

There are two other important concepts[5] when talking about good communication between couples. These concepts are "intent" and "impact." In other words, the message sent does not necessarily equal the message received. Let's look at these concepts:

• **Intent** is the message *intended* by the speaker.

• **Impact** is the message *received* by the listener.

• **Accurate communication** is when *intent* EQUALS *impact*. When intent DOES NOT equal impact, something has distorted the communication process.

- **This distortion is called a "Filter."** Filters can be on the speaker side or on the listener side or both.

Types of Filters

Anything that distorts communication is a type of "filter." The following are some common types of filters:

- **Inattention** – hearing and speech problems, noise in the environment, or just being too tired to communicate well.

- **Emotional States** – bad moods, negative emotions, strong feelings such as anger, sadness, happiness.

- **Beliefs and Expectations** – belief that someone means to hurt you if they raise their voice, belief that silence during an argument means your partner does not care. There are many, many beliefs we bring to our marriage. They are usually learned in our childhood from our family of origin.

  - **Confirmation Bias** – people tend to behave the way we expect them to because we influence their behavior. If we view our spouse either negatively or positively, they tend to live up to our expectations.

  - **Negative Interpretations** – viewing another person more negatively than is truly the case. This causes people to become defensive.

- **Differences in Style** – we all have different styles: wordy or concise, emotional or reserved, dramatic or understated, extrovert or introvert.

- **Self-Protection** – covering up one's real desire or concern out of fear of rejection. ("If I don't state something clearly, you can't reject me as deeply.")

How to Deal with Filters

- Recognize that all kinds of filters become barriers to openness and intimacy in marriage.

- Take responsibility for understanding our own filters.

- Stay in the present. Don't argue about what was said or done in the past when you remember it differently. Deal with the here and now or what you mean...in the present.

- We remember "intent" and "impact" better than actual words.

- Have the humility to NOT ARGUE about whose memory is better.

- Announce your filters when you know they are there. Get them out in the open.

Relevance to Spiritual Relationships

How Good Communication Helps Our Spiritual Life – After reading through the various techniques for developing good communication skills, most of them formulated by secular counselors and psychologists, one may question how this will help the devotee desiring spiritual relationships. First of all, we also know that spiritual life begins with hearing and chanting the names and glories of the Lord – communication of the highest order. Beyond this very spiritual activity of glorifying the Lord with our words, we also know that open and honest communication between Vaishnavas is a virtue. Revealing one's mind in confidence and listening to the confidences of other Vaishnavas is one of our most basic instructions (*Nectar of Instruction* 4).

How We Treat the Lord's Devotees – How do we bring our elevated philosophy of Krishna consciousness into our everyday family life? Well, we know that Lord Krishna is more concerned about how we treat His devotees than about how we treat Him. In other words, when we consider spiritual relationships there is little distinction between the Lord and His devotees. As Lord Krishna advises Arjuna in the *Adi Purana*, "My dear Partha, one who claims to be my devotee is not so. Only a person who claims to be the devotee of my devotees is actually my devotee."[6]

So, how we treat our spouses, who are, after all, devotees of the Lord, becomes very important to our spiritual progress.

When all is said and done, success in a Krishna conscious marriage depends on the willingness and commitment of each partner not only to create an atmosphere where spiritual life can thrive, but to care for each other as Vaishnavas. As we would treat a Vaishnava with honesty, sincerity, care, and respect, so we should treat our spouse and children. Good communication skills promote these virtues and create a peaceful atmosphere in which spiritual life can flourish. And do not forget the powerful influence your role modeling will have on your children and your children's children! Hare Krishna.

About the Author

GVT

MANTRINI DEVI DASI (Mireya Pourchot, BS), a disciple of His Divine Grace A.C. Bhaktivedanta Swami Prabhupada since 1972, is a member of the North American Grihastha Vision Team, a certified PREP© (Preparation and Relationship Enhancement Program) marriage educator, a "Good Touch, Bad Touch"© Trainer and Facilitator, a board member of New Raman Reti (NRR) Mediation Board in Alachua, a board member and secretary of ISKCON of Alachua Temple Management Board, a steering committee member of the NRR Devotee Care Department, and a Reporter/Production Manager for the NRR Weekly Newsletter. Formerly, she was Publicity Manager for the ISKCON Child Protection Office, and board member of Children of Krishna, Inc. She has a bachelor's degree in Child and Family Studies.

Currently, Mantrini devi dasi and her husband, Tamohara dasa, co-facilitate a monthly grihastha training group for young couples, and they meet with individuals and couples for lay counseling in their home in Alachua, Florida, USA. In her free time, Mantrini devi dasi dresses and sews for the Deities of Sri Sri Radha Syamasundara and the murti of Srila Prabhupada at New Raman Reti Dhama. She and her husband have been married for 43 years and have four daughters and three grandchildren.

Chapter 4 Roles of the Husband and Wife in the Vaishnava Community

Tariq Saleem Ziyad

In this chapter you will learn:

- ✓ How to Recognize and Appreciate Gender Differences
- ✓ How to Apply the Principle of Material Differences and Spiritual Equality
- ✓ How Cultural Norms May Affect Your Marriage
- ✓ Factors that Affect the Roles of Husband and Wife
- ✓ How to Negotiate Roles in Your Marriage, based on Time, Place, and Circumstance

Couch potato

Principles Highlighted in this Chapter

- Alignment with Srila Prabhupada

- Spiritual Equality / Material Difference

- Positive and Realistic Vision

- Mutual Respect and Appreciation

- Commitment and Dedication

Introduction

The Age of Kali Increases Conflict in Marriage – In today's world, more than any other time in history, there is a need for information about negotiating the roles and responsibilities in marriage for both husbands and wives. According to the Vedic scriptures, we are currently living in the Age of Kali, a period of irreligion, quarrel, and hypocrisy. This is confirmed by observing the world we live in, which is full of struggle and conflict – within each person as well as between people, countries, and ethnic and religious groups. Thus we see political and social unrest, even leading to war.

Divorces have increased at an alarming rate among all races, religions and cultures. In the United States alone, more than half of all marriages end in divorce, while for second marriages the divorce rates are even higher. Because most couples enter into marriage with little or no preparation or ongoing support, it is no wonder that so many marriages do not last "until death do us part."

The Grihastha Ashrama – This is a book about spiritual family life – the grihastha ashrama – and this chapter will concentrate on how couples can recognize and agree on their roles and responsibilities as husband and wife in relationship to their practice of Krishna consciousness. Some couples begin their marriage with an agreement on their mutual goals, while others leave it up to chance – thinking that mutual attraction is all that is needed. This second approach is dangerous to any marriage. Premarital education with an opportunity to practice skills is essential to help couples clarify their roles and responsibilities. Having agreements and understanding before marriage helps everything and everyone move forward more peacefully.

What Roles are Appropriate? Determining appropriate roles and responsibilities in a Krishna conscious marriage and carrying them out is not a very easy thing to do. Why?

Beside the fact that it is different for each couple, and even for the same couple at different points along the life-cycle, a difficulty arises from trying to adapt a Vedic model of marriage to a very different time and culture. Srila Prabhupada, Founder-*Acharya* of the International Society for Krishna Consciousness, taught us to apply Krishna conscious ideals, including roles and responsibilities, in relationship to the "time (*kala*), place (*desa*), and circumstance (*patra*)." This is a dynamic, sensible idea, which obviously allows scope for different opinions on how to apply it. We have to also take into consideration our individual and collective training, experience, temperament, and our commitment to be Krishna conscious despite obstacles.

Influences from Different Cultures – Devotees who follow Srila Prabhupada's teachings may have challenges in regard to the roles of husband and wife, especially when we take into account influences from:

• Contemporary Western society

• Contemporary Indian society

• Vedic society in India more than 5,000 years ago

• ISKCON the institution

For example, if we grew up in contemporary Western society, our values and understanding of gender roles was likely quite different from modern or traditional Indian society, or for that matter, from what we currently believe and practice when following Srila Prabhupada's teachings.

Cultural Backgrounds Must Be Considered – Consider two married people coming from different backgrounds or cultures. Each person's past living experiences and culture will affect the adjustments they need to make to follow Srila Prabhupada's teachings and their current application in ISKCON. More effort would be required to adjust to one another, with the necessity of making compromises that arise due to different cultural perspectives.

Srila Prabhupada's approach to a Krishna conscious lifestyle did not fit into the Western cultural model or, for that matter, into the cultural model of modern India. It was based on the ideals taught in the Vedic scriptures and applied on the basis of "time, place, and circumstance." After all, lifestyle practices are not ends in themselves, but are meant to serve spiritual principles. Transplanting practices from one place to another without serving the ultimate purpose would have proven to be counterproductive.

Breaking with cultural tradition, Srila Prabhupada allowed women to live in the ashrama and serve in the Temple kitchen and on the altar. He also permitted women to take second initiation, which was previously not widely practiced. To continue this great work of Srila Prabhupada's, we have to catch the spirit behind his adjustments of cultural details without giving up our values and principles. Devotees today are faced with the challenge of understanding how to apply the principles of Krishna consciousness in different cultural settings. We pray to be up to the task!

Our premise is that if we apply the Twelve Principles for Successful Krishna Conscious Family Life, based on Srila Prabhupada's teachings using spiritual common sense, we can accomplish the task!

What did Srila Prabhupada teach us about understanding gender differences?

> Since both the boys and the girls are being trained to become preach-ers, those girls are not ordinary girls but are as good as their brothers who are preaching Krishna consciousness. Therefore, to engage both boys and girls in fully transcendental activities is a policy intended to spread the Krishna consciousness movement.
>
> [*Chaitanya-charitamrita, Adi* 7.31-32, purport]

> A man's psychology and woman's psychology are different. As consti-tuted by bodily frame, a man always wants to be superior to his wife.
>
> [*Srimad-Bhagavatam* 3.23.2, purport]

> So woman should always be engaged to assist the man in every respect in his religious life, in his social life, in his family life. That is real bene-fit of conjugal life. But if the woman does not agree with the man, and the man treats [the] woman as his servant, that is not good. The man should give the woman all protection and the woman should give all service to the man. That is ideal life, family life, conceived in the Vedic way of life.
>
> [*Dialectic Spiritualism*]

Differences Between Men and Women

John Gray authored the book[1] with the title that popularized the saying "Men are from Mars; Women are from Venus." This book and other similar books on com-munication between the genders point out that men and women communicate differently and many times seek different outcomes. Women may want to express themselves and connect with others, while men may want to solve problems.

In his wisdom, Srila Prabhupada pointed out that the psychology of both genders is different. In the roles men and women practiced in traditional marriages of the past, male and female differences were easier to see and experience. Today there are so many changes happening so fast in the present cultures, that many aspects of the different roles have become blended or blurred. Change is occurring so fast that one author[2] called its impact on the mind a "Future Shock."

With intelligent, respectful adjustments according to one's nature and culture, we can still address appropriate gender roles in today's world. The key is to have both husband and wife serve one another in the pursuit of spiritual life using the princi-ples and values established by Srila Prabhupada.

Oneness and Difference – In our philosophy, the concept of simultaneous oneness and difference, *acintya bheda abheda tattva,*[3] is fundamental. Such a concept appears to be difficult to grasp but can more easily be understood when we use the marriage relationship as an example. In a marriage, we have two people who have committed themselves to helping one another in their spiritual lives for the purpose of raising a family and for mutual support. They agree that each will contribute wholly of themselves to support the other partner materially and spiritually, as a couple and as a family – one in spirit – two individuals in harmony for common objectives.

Therefore, from the philosophy of Krishna consciousness, we understand that men and women are both equally qualified to engage in devotional service and can both attain the same heights of service to God and love of God. In other words even though we recognize a "material difference," we also practice a "spiritual equality." As we continue the discussion of the roles of husband and wife, these concepts will be our backdrop.

We can serve the purposes of the grihastha ashrama with the help of the Vedic scriptures, Srila Prabhupada's teachings, current gurus, and association with advanced devotees and respected peers. To do this, we must take into account our culture, family, and personal circumstances, as well as our material necessities and spiritual standing. Through this process, we can find what works best in our marriage, as well as what helps us care for each other and our children in order to practice Krishna consciousness.

We are Not the Body, but Spirit Soul – The most basic spiritual concept we understand is that the real person is not the material body but spirit soul. Although fundamental, it is still difficult to completely realize. Nevertheless, trying to apply this concept helps us gradually rise above the physical differences between people and subsequently understand that we are all equal spiritually.

Once a female devotee approached Srila Prabhupada questioning why she was being treated as a "female." He just asked her the question, "Are you the body?" This question also comes up in the issues of skin color. Again the question becomes, "Are you the body or spirit soul?" Srila Prabhupada wrote one devotee and told her, "If someone mistreats you because of the color of your skin, that's their ignorance. If you accept it, then that's your ignorance." From his statements, we can see it is a form of ignorance to mistreat others based on color, gender, or other bodily conceptions.

Actually, in relationship to Krishna we are all female to be enjoyed by Him, and we are never the master or the enjoyer. In the material world, material maleness or femaleness is only a dress. Of course, we do try to take into consideration the different psychologies of men and women, but we do so only in order to understand our unique conditioning, taking into consideration the cultural and practical situations in which we live.

Whatever our gender, we are taught by Lord Chaitanya that the highest ideal of worship is that exemplified by the *gopis,* the cowherd damsels of Vraja. Each *gopi* assists the other *gopis* in their service to please Krishna. Each *gopi* serves the others in a very cooperative mood. This is the example of how to best serve Krishna by serving His devotees (which include our spouse), who in turn serve the Lord.

Female and Male Physical Differences Defining Roles – Certainly, male and female bodies are physically different, and this should be taken into account. And those physical differences make it possible for the community to perpetuate itself into the future. In other words, this is one way to increase the number of devotees – by having devotee children. In the early stages of our movement, we would primarily proselytize to add new members into our community. Now, in addition to our outreach efforts, by strengthening our families and creating ongoing support for them, we will have stable, vibrant communities, which will in turn attract new members.

Healthy families mean a healthy, fortified community, now and for the future. Because a woman spends several years bearing each child, this does not give her as much time in the early child rearing stages to work outside the home. The husband, therefore, takes on the major responsibility for supporting the family during this period. It is also a common occurrence that wives work fulltime once their children are in school. To facilitate the proper care of children, there is a need for husbands and wives to negotiate the housework and childrearing responsibilities. Also, when living in a Krishna conscious community, parents can share in the care of one another's children, giving parents more time for work or service.

Factors that may affect the duties and roles of householders include:

- Cultural backgrounds, including different religions and ethnic origins

- Professions

- Extended family support

- Whether one or both devotees are new to the practice of Krishna consciousness

- Having children from previous marriages

- Work schedules

Traditional Family Roles – When contemplating whether to adopt traditional family roles, it is important to see that the key to healthy grihastha life is cooperation promoting loving exchanges, thereby serving the principles of Krishna consciousness. Traditional family roles often worked in the past because the surrounding culture and environment were supportive. For example, in these traditional families, the husband's primary role was to provide for and protect family members and often revolved around farmland.

Though we may see such traditional roles as ideal in many ways, we have to deal with the reality of current times and places. This necessitates more of an equal partnership rather than rigid roles that require men to provide all the financial support and require women to do all the work in the home.

Inspiration from Lord Krishna's Example

As devotees, we receive our best inspiration in our practice of Krishna consciousness when we apply the attributes of fine behavior and commitment to the principle of being Krishna conscious in our everyday life. As we study the ideal, we consider how to apply it uniquely, according to our circumstances. In this regard, principles have no gender. Our main principle is to always remember Krishna and never forget Him.

We are also reminded of this in the six principles of surrender given by Srila Bhaktivinoda Thakura. One of the principles of surrender is to accept what is favorable for Krishna consciousness and to give up what is unfavorable. This should be our guiding light in our marriage; this should be the principle around which the various roles and responsibilities revolve.

Srila Prabhupada's books show us how Lord Krishna set the ideal example as a family man, providing each one of His wives with her own palace. When Narada Muni visited, he was amazed at how each queen was fully supported and each one had Krishna's full attention as He enjoyed joking exchanges with them and played with the children. Srila Prabhupada writes:

> The Supreme Personality of Godhead was engaged in His so-called household affairs in order to teach people how one can sanctify one's household life although one may be attached to the imprisonment of material existence. Actually, one is obliged to continue the term of material existence because of household life. But the Lord, being very kind upon householders, demonstrated the path of sanctifying ordinary household life. Because Krishna is the center of all activities, the life of a Krishna conscious householder is transcendental to Vedic injunctions and is automatically sanctified.

> [*Krishna Book*, Chapter 69: The Great Sage Narada
> Visits the Different Homes of Lord Krishna]

Lord Ramachandra is the ideal ruler, husband, and son. His wife Sita devi represents the ideal wife following the lead of her husband with great devotion. They are perfect examples, like spiritual archetypes, which encourage us to understand the ideals they exemplify. Their example may seem unobtainable. However, we can apply their spirit of devotion to one another, adapting their roles in a way that makes sense to us. One of the most important principles is to honor one another – not condemn our faults or failures – and press on in our attempts to live up to the ideal.

Devotees strengthen their resolve to be good followers of Srila Prabhupada by reading and studying the philosophy of Krishna consciousness along with the pastimes. We fortify ourselves with the examples of how Krishna and His devotees serve the principles of a Krishna conscious married life.

Roles of Husband and Wife

One of the main reasons for so many divorces is the breakdown of mutual respect and appreciation. With the lack of appreciation, there is a corresponding loss of respect. As a result, couples may not act responsibly or with the care needed to carry out their various roles effectively. Many male and female roles are taken for granted and that is why we emphasize negotiating to achieve clarity on this and other topics *before marriage.*

Family as the Foundation of Society (a Mini-Government) – In any society, the family is its foundation. The family is a mini-government with each member having roles and responsibilities. This is not as simple as telling everyone to do the same thing. Each family member has to be affectionately committed to support the others. This helps the marriage and family life to flow better, as water flows around obstacles to its ultimate destination. When a couple is supportive of one another's material and spiritual goals, and united in their shared family mission, everyone benefits and Krishna is pleased with the harmonious family atmosphere.

Biases Brought from Our Family of Origin – It is important for couples to realize that each person brings their own ideas or biases about gender roles from their respective family of origin and culture. These role conceptions are so ingrained into the fabric of our being that we may not even be aware of them. We may say when asked, that we don't have any role expectations in marriage, or we may unthinkingly accept the traditional Vedic roles given in scripture without evaluating the important principles and values established by these roles. We assume our partner shares our gender role paradigm, and we don't discuss the subject before marriage. As you might expect, this is a recipe for marital problems. Therefore, it is essential to bring out these unspoken expectations before getting married, and then to come to mutually agreed upon roles and responsibilities. Following the examples in scriptures helps us overcome any bias we might have as they give us the ideal actions in relationships. Of course, in a neophyte stage we may not understand how to apply the ideal to our reality, and so we should take guidance from mature devotees.

Role Assignments – As mentioned before, there are some fundamental basics that apply to both men and women equally. This can best be seen in the spiritual examples outlined above. However, there are other aspects of our roles and responsibilities that can best be carried out according to our particular mind and bodily make up. Additionally, roles may change over time: as we get older, as we change employment, and as children are born or leave the home.

In order to see your assumptions and cultural biases, use the chart below to pick the roles which you think are best assigned to the wives, which to the husbands, and which could be carried out by both. Your spouse or future spouse could try this as well. This could be a basis for discussion and negotiation where the two of you have chosen differently.

Visit VaisnavaFamilyResources.org for a printable version of this chart.

Roles and Responsibilities	Wife	Husband	Both
Provide Economic Resources for Household			
Cook for Family			
Protect Family Members			
Clean the House			
Discipline Children			
Pay the Bills			
Balance the Checkbook			
Transport Children to School			
Take Children to School Events			
Attend Children's School Events			
Invite Guests to the Home			
Care for Guests in the Home			
Lead in Arranging Cultural Activities for the Family			
Assist in Arranging Cultural Activities for the Family			
Make Final Decisions after Consultation with Family			
Act as Head of Family			
Shop for Food			
Set Goals for Family			
Transmit Spiritual & Cultural Traditions			
Nurture Children with Warmth			
Initiate Emotional Exchanges			
Provide Spiritual Leadership			
Choose Where to Reside			
Decide Which Appliances and Furniture to Buy			
Decide When, Where and How Much to Give in Charity			
Create and Maintain Household Routines			
Establish and Maintain Important Family Records – such as Birth Certificates, Passports, and Insurance papers			
Establish and Maintain Important Household Documents – such as Property Deed or Lease, automobile repair records, and warranties			

As demonstrated by the above exercise, couples can best determine their roles using their intelligence, respect, love, and concern for one another, thus cooperating in the mood of service. They can lovingly negotiate these roles so that everything flows nicely. Keep in mind that roles may change over time, as we get older, as we change employment, and as children are born or leave the home. The goal is respectful compromise without compromising principles and values.

Summary

Challenges and Opportunities – We are living in a time of both challenge and opportunity. We have the opportunity to show how the purposes of a Krishna conscious marriage can be applied in a dynamic way in the various cultures throughout the world. As devotee husbands and wives, we can set a good example by demonstrating our ability to define husband and wife roles in marriage reasonably and practically, while acting in accordance with scripture. If we use the Twelve Principles distilled by the Grihastha Vision Team from the teachings of Srila Prabhupada, we will have inspiration and hope to accomplish this purpose.

Although there may be many challenges trying to live in accordance with these principles and values, we increase our chances of success by staying conscious of our ultimate purpose, which is to serve and love Krishna and His dedicated devotees. Since Krishna consciousness is universal, we can apply these principles according to **the time, the place, and the circumstances** in which we find ourselves. If we use our God-given intelligence, our devotion for guru and Krishna, and our love, respect, and concern for one another, we can dutifully serve the purposes of the grihastha ashrama. We do this in part by honoring our natural differences, our talents and expertise, yet acting on our oneness of purpose – the purpose being to return back home, back to our original pure consciousness of Krishna.

Husband and wife are first and foremost Vaishnavas, devotees of Krishna, to be respected, served and assisted by each other. With this in mind, we can support and cooperate with each other in order to best reach our mutual goals. We can arrange our roles and responsibilities to serve these purposes and not just accept rigid stereotypes.

What works, works! We can apply the principle of evaluating by the results: if the purpose of Krishna consciousness is ultimately served, that is success.

My humble prayer for all of us is that we enthusiastically use the many examples in scripture of caring, morality, respect, and courtesy modeled by Lord Krishna and His pure servants to inspire and empower ourselves and others with hope of better outcomes. May we consistently practice these examples in our own lives and continue laying the foundation for a better future.

About the Author

TARIQ SALEEM ZIYAD, BA has been a dedicated supporter of the Hare Krishna community for over 20 years. He is married to Krsnanandini devi dasi, President of the Grihastha Vision Team, and both are Co-Directors of Dasi-Ziyad Family Institute (www.dzfi.org). As a founding member of the Cleveland Nama Hatta Program, he gives support in time, money, and meeting space for the development of the Hare Krishna community in Cleveland, Ohio. Tariq is a member of the North American Grihastha Vision Team, a Certified Family Life Educator (CFLE), a Certified PREP© Administrator (Preparation and Relationship Enhancement Program), and a Certified Family Wellness Instructor. Tariq has degrees in Psychology and Business Management from Baldwin-Wallace College, Berea, Ohio.

Chapter 5 Krishna's Economics: Spiritualizing Your Wealth

Arcana Siddhi devi dasi

In this chapter you will learn:

✓ How Our Family of Origin Shapes Our Attitudes About Money

✓ The Foundation of the Grihastha Ashrama: the Spirit of Giving

✓ The Principles of Krishna's Economics

✓ How to Create a Budget

Half Baked
© David Musterer

Principles Highlighted in this Chapter

• Positive and Realistic Vision

• Personal and Social Responsibility

• Economic Development and Prosperity

Is Money the Root of All Evil?

Money is Personified as the Goddess of Fortune – Many of us who grew up in the Western world have heard the biblical quote "Love of money is the root of all evil."[5] Money is God's energy – personified as Laksmi devi, the Goddess of Fortune. How can the Lord's energy be considered the root of all evil?

Most of us are familiar with Lord Ramachandra's pastime where the evil King Ravana kidnaps Rama's chaste and beautiful wife, Sita devi, hoping to enjoy her for himself. Sita devi is none other than Laksmi devi appearing on earth to assist her Lord in pastime adventure. What we can learn from this most instructive pastime, or *lila*, is that when we try to enjoy Laksmi devi separate from her Lord, we take on the characteristics of Ravana, who was full of greed and envy. Despite having opulence greater than the King of Heaven, his heart burned with lust. In a similar way, if we try to enjoy the kingdom of God without God, we will never find happiness, and our consciousness will become more and more degraded.

Yukta-Vairagya – On the other hand, when Laksmi devi is engaged in the Lord's service, she becomes very satisfied and happy; thus we become satisfied and happy. Sometimes, in our immature spiritual development, we think we should renounce things of this world including money. However, Srila Prabhupada taught us a different principle: *yukta-vairagya,* using everything in Krishna's service. Once, the devotees showed Srila Prabhupada a picture of a famous yogi refusing the riches offered to him by his admirers. When Prabhupada saw this picture, he opened his arms widely indicating his complete acceptance of the riches and said, "Give it to me; I will use it for Krishna." So love of money with the vision to use it in the Lord's service will liberate us, not degrade us.

Understanding our Attitudes about Money

Attitudes about Money Affect our Marriage – Most devotees who enter the grihastha ashrama also have to be concerned with making money to support the needs of a family. While money is a necessity, it is the attitudes we carry about money into our marriage that can have a profound effect on the health of our relationship with our spouse. Money frequently represents security, enjoyment, status, power, and freedom. Because we grew up in a culture that often equates money with happiness, the issue of money can come between spouses when there are disagreements about how money should be spent and saved.

In some relationships, one spouse may use money to control and have power over the other spouse. Some years ago I counseled a couple where the husband refused to give his wife access to their bank account or credit cards. Whenever she needed to buy anything she had to go to her husband and ask for money. Because of this arrangement, she developed more and more resentment towards him. By the time they came to see me, it was "too little, too late." She ended up leaving the marriage.

I saw another couple where the husband couldn't control his spending habits. He put thousands of dollars on credit cards and he would hide the statements from his wife. They eventually were forced to declare bankruptcy. In this case the couple worked together to put their lives back together, and the husband got individual help for his compulsive spending.

Issues concerning money are one of the principle stressors in a marriage. If left unresolved, they can destroy the loving bond between two people and lead to divorce.

Attitudes about Wealth May Differ between Spouses – Before couples can be successful in keeping a budget and having short term and long term financial goals, they need to be aware of the attitudes and beliefs they hold about money. For instance, I grew up in a family where my mother had deep fears about lack and limitation of resources. Once when I asked her to buy a dress for me, she became distraught and said, "Go ahead; I'll just be a bag lady in my old age!" Of course, I didn't buy the dress – instead, a piece of her fear about spending money entered into my psyche. My father, on the other hand, was quite the opposite. He was generous, spent money without fear, and always had faith that money would come. Interestingly enough, my father's father came to the United States from Poland at the age of 12 years-old. He came alone and didn't speak any English. Despite these challenges, he made a life for himself and prospered. On the other hand, my mother's parents both came from families that had wealth and lost that wealth during the Great Depression.

So, we can get a glimpse into how our beliefs and attitudes about money are shaped by our family of origin. When we join together in marriage, our money paradigms can clash with one another and can become a source of constant pain. Sometimes I would see my mother deeply upset after my father would purchase something my mother didn't think was necessary, such as a new car every three to four years. My mother would have kept the car for at least 10 years!

Children Imbibe the Attitudes of the Parents – As a result of my upbringing, I carried both my mother and father's attitudes about money into my adult life. I vacillated between my father's generosity and my mother's fears around spending money. In the early years of our marriage, Karnamrita and I didn't have much discretionary income, so I would get upset when he would buy books, since I felt he could borrow them from the library. My husband, however, placed high value on owning books. We were able to find a compromise where he would limit his book buying. I am lucky to be married to someone who allows me to share my feelings and who is willing to find a mutually satisfying solution.

I also have had the great fortune of being molded by Krishna conscious experiences. More and more, I try to imbibe the realization that money is Laksmi devi, the constant companion and consort of the Lord. As devotees in the grihastha ashrama, this understanding is crucial to our success in this ashrama. The duty of the grihastha ashrama is to give in charity.

"Give to Live"

Giving in Charity – One time while on a morning walk with Srila Prabhupada, a devotee inquired from him about the essence of grihastha life. Srila Prabhupada replied, "To be married in Krishna consciousness means that before you eat your *prasadam*, you go out in the street and you call three times loudly, 'Does anyone want to take *prasadam*? Does anyone want to take *prasadam*? Does anyone want to take *prasadam*?' If no one comes, then you take your *prasadam*." The devotee asking the question was a little bewildered by this answer and thought, "Perhaps Prabhupada didn't understand the question." He again asked Srila Prabhupada the same question, "What is the essence of grihastha life?" Again Srila Prabhupada repeated the same answer.[2]

When I first heard this story, I thought deeply about Prabhupada's reply to this devotee who had just entered the grihastha ashrama. I realized that the propensity of the living entity in the material condition is to think in terms of "I, me and mine." To make advancement in spiritual pursuits, it is necessary to go beyond this selfish conception and to think about the spiritual and material welfare of others. One of the principles of householder life is to generate wealth and prosperity by ethical means. This is because giving in charity is an essential duty for the grihastha ashrama. Householder life means to become a giver – ultimately to give everything in the service of the Lord. This is what Srila Prabhupada was trying to illustrate by saying that the essence of grihastha life is giving in charity.

Understanding the Principles of Krishna's Economics

Material Economies Go Through Cycles of Dualities – Throughout history, the economy goes through cycles. Generally, economic downturn is a result of excessive greed and exploitation. So, should anyone be surprised about the current state of affairs? If we are immersed in a mentality of enjoying separately from the Lord in this material plane of existence, then we are subjected to the laws that govern this world.

We know from the *Bhagavad-gita* that everything in this realm is full of duality: happiness and distress, loss and gain, victory and defeat. We also know that everything is temporary. This is a recipe for mental anxiety which is always heightened during difficult times. However, those individuals who have taken to the path of devotion to God are under a different set of rules – Krishna's economics where "one minus one equals one."

Krishna's Economics – Srila Prabhupada tells a very nice story[3] to illustrate this principle of "one minus one equals one." Once, there was a young boy in India who came from a very poor family. He was a student in the *gurukula,* the guru's school, and his teacher was hosting a big festival for the community. The teacher asked all of his students to bring some food preparation for this event. When the boy went home and asked his mother what he could bring, she told him they were too poor and couldn't contribute anything. The little boy began to sob. Seeing her son in such a distressed condition, she advised that he go to forest and find Dina Bandhu, a name for Krishna meaning "the friend of the poor."

Feeling some hope, the little boy went to the forest calling out loudly, "Dina Bandhu, please come; Dina Bandhu, please come." After some time of this earnestly petitioning, the Lord finally appeared before the small child. Upon hearing of his plight, the Lord told him to tell his teacher that he would bring yogurt for the festival. The Lord instructed him to return to the forest on the day of the event, and He would give him the yogurt.

The teacher was very pleased to hear that the child would supply the yogurt for the festival. On the morning of that special day, the little boy went to the forest again calling for his Lord to come. The Lord appeared with a container of yogurt, and the small boy happily went to school with his treasure.

However, when the teacher saw that the boy had brought only a small container of yogurt, he became angry, saying "What, you have only brought this much yogurt? There will be hundreds of people attending our festival."

In his anger the teacher knocked the container from the boy's grip, and it spilled out onto the floor. When the teacher picked up the container, he was amazed to see it was still full of yogurt. He again spilled the yogurt and to his astonishment, it remained full. He could then realize that laws governing the yogurt were spiritual and not material.

Lord Krishna Will Carry What We Lack and Preserve What We Have – The above principle explains how there can never be a recession in the spiritual world. If we take shelter of the Lord of the spiritual world, we will be protected from any lack or limitation. Krishna tells us in the *Bhagavad-gita* that He will preserve what a fully surrendered devotee has, and He will provide what he lacks (*Bhagavad-gita* 9:22). So, to the degree that we are dedicating our life to the Lord, to that degree He will take care of all of our needs.

Miraculous Stories of Krishna Providing – Over the years, devotees have had many experiences that verify Krishna's promise to provide and take care of His devotees. In the very early days of Srila Prabhupada's mission, the devotees in San Francisco didn't have any money for their rent and were facing eviction. The morning of their impending eviction, they were leaving their apartment to go down the street for the morning service at the Temple. They had no idea how to pay the rent. As they came outside, they saw that one-hundred-dollar bills were floating down from an undetectable source! The devotees gathered up the money and were able to pay their rent and give a sizable donation to Srila Prabhupada. When they told Srila Prabhupada the source of the unexpected money, Srila Prabhupada was not a bit surprised.[4]

Another time the devotees in Philadelphia were in a similar situation. The rent was due, and they had no money. They decided to continue their regular spiritual service of *harinama sankirtana,* singing mantras glorifying the Lord to the public, and depend on Krishna's mercy. That day, a man they had never seen (and never saw again) came up to the chanting party and handed them an envelope that said "For Krishna." The exact amount of the rent due was inside the envelope!

In both these examples, Krishna placed the devotees in a situation where their only recourse was to depend on the Lord. Sometimes the Lord may place the devotee in a difficult situation just to prove that He is the source of their supply. In this way, the devotees' faith becomes stronger, and they become free from anxiety in future distressful situations, knowing that Krishna will provide for all their needs.

The More We Use Resources in Krishna's Service, the More He Provides – Another principle in Krishna's economics is that the more a devotee is able to utilize the resources he is given in the Lord's service, the more facility and resources he will be provided. Srila Prabhupada exemplified this principle in his outreach efforts after coming to the United States in 1965. In just a few short years, Srila Prabhupada had over 100 temples and centers throughout the world with so many resources to spread Lord Chaitanya's mission.

The opposite is also true. If we misuse resources meant to be used in the Lord's service, then He may restrict our assets or take them away. If, as a result of having material wealth, a person forgets about their service to the Lord, then out of love for that person, the Lord can confiscate that wealth. Krishna protects His fledgling devotees from becoming enamored or proud from having too many material possessions.

When We Give, We Get – Another important tenet of Krishna's economics is that when we give, we get. Krishna tells us in the *Bhagavad-gita* that as we surrender to Him, He reciprocates accordingly. Money, time, our labor, and our material attachments are all things we can give to the Lord, and He will reciprocate beyond our greatest expectations. The scriptures contain many stories to support this principle. In *Srimad-Bhagavatam,* there is a story of Krishna going out to barter with a fruit vendor. Playing the part of a toddler, He held some grains in His small hands. But, by the time He reached the vendor, most of the grains had slipped through His tiny fingers, and He had almost nothing left to give her. Seeing the Lord's enchanting effulgent face, the fruit vendor felt love in her heart for the child. She piled His arms full of fruits. In exchange the Lord filled her basket with valuable jewels.

Heart & Soul Connection

Mercantile Relationships with the Lord – We shouldn't enter into a mercantile relationship with Krishna thinking that 'I will give so much to the Lord, and I will get back so much.' While it is true that Krishna may fulfill our desires in this way, we will be missing out on the real "getting" which is getting love for the Lord. We should give to the Lord in a mood of service and beg to be able to participate in eternal service. In the eternal reality, everything is perpetually provided, and there is no anxiety over how to maintain our bodies.

Inspired by the Pure Devotees – We can be inspired by pure devotees who have no desire for anything beyond the bare necessities of keeping the body, mind, and soul together. Their consciousness is merged in the transcendent reality where there is unlimited wealth, and where there are trees that fulfill any desire. Yet the residents of that reality only desire things for serving Radha and Krishna. They eat sumptuous rich food, not for sense gratification but because it makes Krishna happy. They wear beautiful clothing and ornaments only to make Krishna happy – the wealth of the devotee is a pure ever-increasing emotion of love for the Lord.

Krishna's Stimulus Package – If we apply these principles into our lives, we too will enter into a consciousness where Krishna's economics prevail. Even while living in this world, we can become free of our material conditioning. Krishna's stimulus package for the present times is to chant His holy names, *Hare Krishna, Hare Krishna, Krishna Krishna, Hare Hare; Hare Rama, Hare Rama, Rama Rama, Hare Hare*. These names will purify our heart of desires for things that separate us from loving Krishna. This formula of chanting has the potency to bring peace and prosperity into our marital relationship.

Keeping Krishna in the Center – Sometimes, we see devotees enter the grihastha ashrama and, because of time restraints, they gradually decrease their spiritual practices. They become more focused on making money and less interested in developing their relationship with Krishna. This is a poor solution to economic problems. Laksmi devi is very fickle without the presence of her Lord Krishna. And rather than increase one's prosperity, one will become both materially and spiritually bereft. Keeping Krishna in the center of our lives is the way to true everlasting prosperity.

Couple's Exercise

There are four areas of difficulty that couples may encounter when trying to develop a financial plan. As a couple, review these common financial planning pitfalls and honestly assess to what degree they may be present in your relationship:

1. **Values Conflict** – The two of you may not agree on the relative value or importance of certain specific goals. It is important to prioritize your goals together.

2. **Unrealistic Goals** – If expectations are unrealistic, debt will be incurred along with stress and frustration. For example, you may expect the same standard of living as your parents. However, your parents or other older couples worked

for many years to achieve their current standard of living. Your goals need to be realistic and achievable.

3. **Emotional Use of Money** – There may be hidden meaning attached to the use of money. The motivation could be to spend money in exchange for status or friendship, or to meet emotional needs for love, security, or power. It is crucial to recognize that money can be used inappropriately in an attempt to meet emotional needs.

4. **Lack of Planning** – We need to establish spending plans to meet our financial goals. Without a plan, we are more susceptible to such things as impulse spending, inadequate insurance, overuse of credit cards, and overdue bills.

After you and your spouse have a discussion about the above pitfalls, try responding to the following questions individually, and then discuss your answers together.

- What was your mother's relationship with money?

- What was your father's relationship with money?

- How were you affected by their beliefs about money?

- How would you describe your relationship with money?

- Has your belief about money caused conflict in your marriage?

- If so, how?

- How would you like your relationship with money to be?

- What steps can you take to get to your ideal?

Creating a Budget

Work Together on a Budget – One of the most important aspects of budgeting as a couple is to do it *as a couple*. Both spouses should feel that their needs and financial goals are considered when an actual budget is created. Budget worksheets of all varieties can be found on the Internet, such as the free downloads at DaveRamsey.com or at GailVazOxlade.com/resources/interactive_budget_worksheet.html. Generally, worksheets include areas for

- fixed monthly expenses such as rent

- variable monthly expenses such as groceries

- occasional expenses such as clothing and repairs

In order to get an accurate picture of your spending baseline for variable and occasional expenses, it is important to carefully track all expenditures for at least three months. While this can be a tedious task, it will prove to be of great value in the end.

Once you have the data regarding your household expenses, both spouses should meet to discuss setting up a budget. Together, you will both need to agree on the amount of money you want to give in charity and put into savings. You will also need to agree on short term and long term financial goals such as buying a house or saving for the children's college tuition.

Live Within Your Means – From counseling couples over the years, I have seen that many of the struggles from finances come from having a very narrow margin between income and expenses, with no allowance for savings. Inevitably, unexpected expenses will show up every month. This means that such couples end up putting more and more on credit cards to cover the expenses. Over a period of time, the mounting credit card debt with high interest rates becomes a source of stress for the couple.

Oftentimes, these same couples made choices to live in a more expensive dwelling and drive a more expensive car than their budget could comfortably handle. In today's world it is easy to become enamored of these amenities without understanding the consequences on our mental health and marital relationship. The old adage "live within your means" should be a guiding principle for everyone, especially devotees who are trying to have time and energy to devote to their spiritual practices.

In Conclusion

Srila Prabhupada also told us that Laksmi devi will personally come and reside in a devotee home where there are harmonious dealings between the husband and the wife.[5] This should be another impetus to work together to address any current or potential financial issues in your marriage. It is never too late to examine our attitudes and behaviors around spending and saving money to ensure they are healthy and in alignment with our spiritual values.

About the Author

ARCANA SIDDHI DEVI DASI (Anne Cox, BSc, MSW) is a disciple of His Divine Grace A. C. Bhaktivedanta Swami Prabhupada. She has a bachelor of science degree in psychology and a master's in clinical social work. She joined the movement in 1976 while in graduate school. She lived and served in the Potomac, Maryland Temple for twelve years, and her main service was book distribution. After moving out of the Temple, she finished her master's degree and worked in a mental health clinic for 14 years, counseling both children and adults.

She is currently living in Prabhupada Village, North Carolina, with her husband, Karnamrita dasa. She has a private practice counseling individuals, couples, and families. She and her husband actively participate in ISKCON as members of the Grihastha Vision Team (GVT). She travels and teaches personal growth seminars, facilitates *japa* retreats, and is a frequent contributor to *Back to Godhead* magazine.

Chapter 6 Affection and Physical Intimacy: The "Hot Potato"

Partha dasa

In this chapter you will learn:

- ✓ The Importance of Affection in Spiritual Life and Marriage
- ✓ How Couples Develop Healthy Attitudes Toward Affection and Connection
- ✓ How Men and Women have Different Approaches to Connection
- ✓ Behaviors and Attitudes that Foster Connection and Fester Disconnection
- ✓ The Regulative Principle Regarding Sex Along with Different Opinions and Conclusions in Relationship to its Application
- ✓ Factors that Put Stress on Connection
- ✓ The Importance of Respectfully and Compassionately Understanding Each Other's Needs

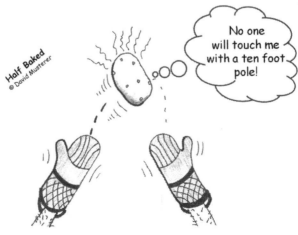

The Hot Potato

Principles Highlighted in this Chapter

- Mutual Respect and Appreciation
- Commitment and Dedication
- Family Love and Affection
- Open and Honest Communication
- Spiritual Equality / Material Difference

First Things First

Reading This Book from the Beginning – If you have skipped ahead to this chapter, remember that just as you cannot make a home run without making it to first base, so you may want to read the previous chapters first. Reading this book from the start will help you to get in touch with and nurture your important values, negotiate cultural and social norms, and be the best, most lovable person you can be. To be loveable, you must love yourself. Loving yourself means becoming the best person you can be. God is supremely lovable, and we are part of Him, so in that sense we are lovable, and especially so if we are trying to be Krishna conscious.

Many marital difficulties can be minimized or solved simply by being in tune with one's own values. Our personal happiness depends on the degree to which we actually live our important values. Marriage is about helping your spouse connect with his or her most important values, as well as the two of you connecting with and living your joint values. Doing so creates security and deep emotional intimacy. Assimilating the previous chapters, especially the chapter on communication skills, will help you and your spouse attain a secure platform to negotiate sensitive topics including sex and intimacy.

Intimacy is a broad topic; please read on with attention and patience.

What did Srila Prabhupada teach us about the importance of affection?

> In the material world, *rajo-guna* is passion, but in the spiritual world it is affection. In the material world, affection is contaminated by *rajo-guna*, but in the *shuddha-sattva* the affection that maintains the devotees is transcendental.
>
> [*Srimad-Bhagavatam* 10.13.50, purport]

To cut off the tie of all other affections does not mean complete negation of the finer elements, like affection for someone else. This is not possible. A living being, whoever he may be, must have this feeling of affection for others because this is a symptom of life. The symptoms of life, such as desire, anger, hankerings, feelings of attraction, etc., cannot be annihilated.

[*Srimad-Bhagavatam* 1.8.42, purport]

From these statements it is evident that affection and love are integral aspects, or needs, of the soul and an essential part of spiritual reality. We can easily deduce that affection is the symptom of life in a Vaishnava marriage.

Paradigms on Intimacy and Their Effects

"Paradigms" or Mental Maps: Our consciousness is like a sponge, continually absorbing impressions and information from our surroundings. Some impressions are very beneficial to our consciousness, such as reading the books written by Srila Prabhupada, the Founder-*Acharya* of the International Society for Krishna Consciousness, or associating with advanced devotees. However, some impressions become negative or detrimental.

Over time all these impressions mold our consciousness, which is to say that they create paradigms which influence our thoughts and behavior. A paradigm can be compared to a mental map. Like it or not, if we are exposed to modern media we imbibe its maps. Modern media portrays love in a rather simplistic manner – passion and sex. The media's main concern is attracting advertising dollars rather than portraying reality. The nature of flat screen media is such that it cannot portray subtle emotional exchanges. Many things which make a marriage successful and fulfilling are subtle; trying to portray them in a movie would be like making a film about paint drying.

Modern Portrayal of Love and Intimacy in the Media: The *Srimad-Bhagavatam* predicted[1] that in the Age of Kali, the age of quarrel and hypocrisy, the finer sentiments of mankind will be lost.

Television is the perfect instrument for attaining that end. Movies are portraying more and more graphic violence, passion, and explicit sexual material to attract the attention of the increasingly jaded senses of the populace. Exposing oneself to this kind of "entertainment" dulls finer sentiments and creates false expectations and conceptions (paradigms or maps) regarding love and intimacy. Is it any wonder that since the advent of television, society has become increasingly self-centered and divorce rates have gone through the roof? One may be looking for a heart-to-heart Krishna conscious connection but have the wrong maps.

Are Your Paradigms on Affection Worth More than 20 Cents?

For example, let's do a little experiment with your understanding (paradigm) of the word "conjugal." Please at least mentally fill in the blank.

The word conjugal implies_____

For most people the connotation of "conjugal" is narrowed to an overly sexual meaning. The actual definition, taken from the Oxford Pocket Dictionary, is:

"of marriage, between married persons."

Then, we might ask what is '*of marriage*' and what goes on '*between married persons*'? Below is a partial list:

Shopping	Praying for a car	Picking up kids toys
Working	Paying for a car	Picking up kids toys again
Negotiating Household duties	Building or renting a house	Raising children
	Fixing the plumbing	Raising teenagers
Private conversations	Shoveling snow	Paying student loans
Exchanging joking words	Chopping wood	Doing laundry
Honoring prasadam	Paying bills	Expressing appreciation
Honoring differences	Having children by sex, adoption, or mystic yoga	Exchanging physical affection
Mowing the lawn		
Tending the garden	Changing diapers	Revealing one's mind
Cleaning the house	Changing lots of diapers	Playfully teasing each other
Ironing clothes	In case of twins, lots and lots and lots of diapers	Going on vacations
		Doing dishes

At first glance it might seem unlikely that many of these items could remotely be considered as conjugal activities, but let us explore that a little more deeply.

> There are two kinds of burdens. There is the burden of the beast and the burden of love. The burden of the beast is unbearable, but the burden of love is a source of pleasure.
>
> [*Srimad-Bhagavatam* 3.3.14, purport]

Thus any of the above activities should be seen and appreciated as an exchange of service and an offering of love. In marriage, these exchanges of service have a subtle meaning or significance when performed in the right consciousness or state of connection. These seemingly small interactions, when performed in the proper awareness, are actually an important element of loving, healthy marriages.

Hot Tip: Appreciating and expressing appreciation for these activities is an empowering act of affection.

Very Hot Tip: Failure to recognize and express such appreciation can wear away the sense of connection and, over time, generate resentment.

My wife has been baking bread regularly since we had our first child 30 years ago. I recently expressed to her how my mother never bought bread but baked her own, and I remembered as a child coming home and smelling freshly baked bread. I told my wife that when I come home and smell the bread that she bakes, it gives me a warm fuzzy feeling like when I was a child. She was quite moved by that, more than if I had just said, "Nice bread!"

Intimacy

Love Connection – We all long for meaningful heart-to-heart connections. In the beginning of marriage, that connection (love) is very profoundly and easily felt. As time goes on, we may become familiar and casual about our relationship, and that feeling or connection can erode.

> Take a few moments every day to express, in a meaningful way, appreciation for something your spouse does in your relationship. Appreciate how that action enhances your life.
>
> Marriage is like the stock market: we do not want it to depreciate but rather, appreciate. The choice is ours.

It is very important to remember that love is a verb, which implies the actions of giving, caring, sacrifice, nurturing, acting with empathy, and so on. The emotion of love is the fruit of these activities. Most couples experience a reduction in this feeling at some point in their relationship. The diminution of that feeling should be viewed as you would the gas gauge on your car. When it gets low, you fill it up.

When you are not feeling love – it is a signal to fill your life with more giving, caring, sacrifice, nurturing, and empathy. Often couples sit in the parking lot of dissatisfaction, the gauge on empty, waiting for their spouse to change. Even just one of you making an attempt to act lovingly will improve the situation.

Intimate Apples, Intimate Oranges

Men and women have different needs, which, when met, help them to feel connected. According to Ayurvedic scripture,[2] those differences help make marriages healthy. Differences simply have to be honored and respected. Be introspective about what you need to feel connected, and be inquisitive about what your spouse needs to feel connected.

Gateways to Intimacy and Connection

Three important portals on the journey to a heart to heart connection are emotional, intellectual, and physical.

Emotional Intimacy

Have you ever tried to put sacred clay, *tilaka,* on your forehead without a mirror? Personally, I have tried this on different occasions, but immediately looked in a mirror to ensure that I did not look like a three year old. Ladies cannot live without mirrors, and every man has at least a tiny mirror for shaving and putting on *tilaka.* Things are lot easier when you can see your reflection. In the same way, processing our thoughts, aspirations, and emotions becomes much easier and clearer when we can see them reflected off the heart of someone in confidence. Srila Rupa Goswami, the author of *Nectar of Instruction,* recommends this as one of his six loving exchanges.

Revealing one's mind in confidence is very crucial for one's spiritual life and marriage. Men, if you have not grasped the principle of open and honest communication and reflective listening, go back and thoroughly study the chapter on communication, Chapter 3. Get coaching on this life skill if necessary. Emotionally connecting with your wife will fulfill one of her most important needs for connection, intimacy and protection. Being able to mutually share and express your feelings, aspirations, frustrations, realizations, appreciations, and needs in a positive, constructive manner is the foundation for connection in marriage and a key to love being manifest.

> *Guhyam akhyati prcchati.* And you disclose your mind; there is no secrecy between the lover and the beloved. And the other party also discloses. In this way, love becomes manifest.
>
> [Lecture on *Chaitanya-charitamrita, Madhya* 20.101, Washington, DC, 6 July 1976]

Differences Between Men and Women – Generally, emotional connection is not as primary a need for men as it is for most women. Sometimes men feel pressured when requested to emotionally connect. One reason is that men often need to feel appreciation and affection in order to connect. Women, on the other hand, cannot even begin to think about being affectionate or appreciative unless they feel emotionally connected. *How's that for a conundrum?*

Ironically, men, when they feel connected, will automatically open up emotionally. And as soon as women feel emotionally connected, they become appreciative and affectionate. If you understand that you are both looking for the same thing, connection (in the form of empathy, being fully present, affection or protection), the process becomes a lot easier.

Hot Tip for Women – If you find that you are frequently pursuing your husband to emotionally connect, and you find that he continually withdraws, and you become increasingly frustrated, please note that one definition of insanity is "repeatedly doing a thing which does not work over and over – expecting a different result." Have compassion for his need for connection, and express your needs in an appreciative, loving way.

Hot Tip for Men – If you observe your wife being frequently frustrated by your attempts to help solve her problems, and you find yourself bewildered and shutting off, and the both of you become increasingly frustrated, please note that one definition of insanity is "repeatedly doing a thing which does not work over and over – expecting a different result." Understand and have compassion for her need for emotional connection, and express your needs in an appreciative, loving way.

Very Hot Tip for Men – Your simple act of connecting with loving empathy is more meaningful and valuable to your wife than you can imagine. That's how much you mean to her.

Very Hot Tip for Women – Expressing appreciation regularly for how much your husband's empathy means to you and enhances your life will help improve and protect your connection.

Okay, But Who's Going to Make the First Move?

Ritual of Connection – Over the years, my wife and I developed what you might call a ritual of connection. It took time, effort, and even some trial and error. We learned to understand and honor each other's needs. Our roads to connection may have been different, but we saw that our common goal was to be intimately connected in our Krishna conscious practices.

One evening recently, some of the teen age girls in our community taught us the ballroom dancing they had just learned. We had not done that since high school more than 40 years ago. Needless to say, it was awkward at first. Believe me, when you both try moving forward, it just does not work! The goal was waltzing, not bumping into each other in an attempt to prove who was right. In a short time though, we were waltzing together smoothly. Developing our connection ritual was a similar experience.

Like many people, my wife is expressive with her hands when she talks. At times she would wave her hand in front of me, or tap my arm as she expressed herself. I could totally understand that she was looking for connection through empathy, but brother! The tapping made me feel like a decaf coffee table! It would make me feel tense and withdrawn. To be honest, it took me some time and introspection to realize that I needed gentle touch to feel connection, a hand **on** the shoulder, or a hug. For me, the difference was like night and day; it allowed me to feel relaxed and grounded, and it opened me to her emotional needs. Over time we learned to understand our own and each other's needs for connection.

Our connection ritual has developed into coming together for a few minutes at various junctions in our day – after our morning program, before leaving for work, when coming home, after dinner, and before taking rest at night – to express our appreciation for some small thing one of us has done and how that gesture enhanced our life.

Take the time to develop your own connection ritual. To be a ritual it should be done regularly, with purpose. Concentrate on the goal of connection and making your differences complement each other. Think of this as the active bond in your marriage vow and an important responsibility to your family, community, guru, Krishna, and yourselves.

Intellectual Intimacy

Sharing your Krishna conscious realizations, inspirations and aspirations is an important bond in a Vaishnava marriage. Lord Krishna describes this activity as a source of bliss.

> The thoughts of My pure devotees dwell in Me, their lives are surrendered to Me, and they derive great satisfaction and bliss enlightening one another and conversing about Me.
>
> [*Bhagavad-gita* 10.9]

Unfulfilled needs for emotional and physical intimacy can create subtle resentment or filters which can in turn obstruct the ability of couples to connect on a meaningful Krishna conscious intellectual platform. If you feel such a block, it is a signal that you need to work on connecting heart to heart. On occasion, Uttama and I have had to work through some issue or challenge. We are very conscientious to reveal our hearts and hear each other. The process never fails to bring us to a deeper level of connection, and we end up in deep, meaningful, enlivening Krishna conscious philosophical discussions.

Physical Intimacy

Sometimes, there is a fear that if physical affection is shown in marriage it may lead to "illicit sex." It is important to note, as stated previously, that affection is a symptom of life. Abstaining from affection will not help anyone advance in Krishna consciousness. One's concern about coming to the highest standard will help one progress; however, abnegating affection in the name of advancement is crippling. Affection and connection is an issue that every couple should negotiate with compassion, honesty, and respect.

Put on your pot holders – in the following sections we will toss this "hot potato" subject around.

Disconnection

My observation from over 40 years in ISKCON is that we have an extremely high rate of divorce and marital dissatisfaction. To a large degree, this is due to a breakdown of affection and connection.

A few examples:

- Women may become reluctant to show affection (touch, hugs) because it may lead to other "illicit things."

- Men become reluctant to emotionally connect with their spouses because they may feel some physical attraction and/or they fear that they may be rejected because of that attraction.

- They both become reluctant to express appreciation and/or affection because it may be taken as a come-on or lead to a 'fall down.'

Such scenarios, devoid of connection, appreciation, and affection (which are needs of the soul) can become recipes for disaster. Unfortunately, this unfulfilled need may cause one or both to look for affection elsewhere, resulting all too often in extramarital affairs, separation, and/or divorce.

Band Aid Solutions

Some sannyasis or gurus will compassionately advise their disciples to concede to marital sex considering that maintaining marriage vows is a priority. However, simply having sex does not guarantee a stable happy marriage.

What I am getting at is that in the sacred institution of marriage, couples should be focused on "connection" with the understanding that the sex issue is one part of a much bigger picture. And as much as the sex concern is a component of the picture, so also, are emotional connection, intellectual connection, and affection.

It is extremely important for couples to look at intimacy and connection with a holistic approach. As stated by Srila Prabhupada, "…then both of them remain fully satisfied, and then they can improve their real business, spiritual understanding." (*Discussion with Hayagriva on Auguste Comte*)

What is Illicit Sex?

Different 'Sloks'[3] For Different Folks – A brahmachari is a student monk who has vowed to be celibate until he changes to the grihastha ashrama; a sannyasi has vowed celibacy for the rest of his life. For either of them, talking with a woman in a secluded place and exchanging joking words would be considered subtle but illicit sex in the strictest sense.

For a householder with his wife, this should be a normal course of affairs.

"My dear beautiful wife, you know that because we are householders we are always busy in many household affairs and long for a time when we can enjoy some joking words between us. That is our ultimate gain in household life." Actually, householders work very hard day and night, but all fatigue of the day's labor is minimized as soon as they meet, husband and wife together, and enjoy life in many ways. Lord Krishna wanted to exhibit Himself as being like an ordinary householder who delights himself by exchanging joking words with his wife.

[*Krishna Book*, Chapter 60: Talks Between Krishna and Rukmini]

Regularly laughing together is an ideal for household life and a symptom of a healthy marriage as indicated by the above quote. Again, the words 'intimacy' and 'conjugal' mean more than just sexual intercourse.

How often do you and your spouse laugh together?

a) daily

b) once or twice a week

c) less than once a week

d) very infrequently

e) cannot remember the last time

The Standard for Physical Intimacy

We understand that the highest standard for physical intimacy in marriage is intercourse performed as a samskara, a purificatory ritual, once in a month for the procreation of children, after chanting 50 rounds at the time conception is most likely to occur.

Those who strictly follow the rules and regulations of householder life engage in sex only once a month, at the end the menstrual period.

[*Srimad-Bhagavatam* 5.13.4, purport]

Although he has a wife, a householder should not use his senses for sex life unnecessarily. There are restrictions for the householders even in sex life, which should only be engaged in for the propagation of children. If he does not require children, he should not enjoy sex life with his wife.

[*Bhagavad-gita* 16.1-3, purport]

The Standard? Yeah, But...

There are opinions in the Vaishnava community that grihasthas have a license for sense enjoyment, and that sex in marriage is permitted, based on statements such as:

> So woman, sex, there is sex, sexual necessity and the bodily demand. So woman not only gives the sex pleasure to the man, but woman should prepare good foodstuff also for the man. The man is working very hard. When he comes home, if the wife supplies him good foodstuff and nice comfort and sex, then the home becomes very happy. That is practical experience. So after hard working, when man comes home, if he finds out good foodstuff and nicely satisfied by eating, and then the woman gives satisfaction by sex, then both of them remain fully satisfied, and then they can improve their real business, spiritual understanding, because human life is meant for making progress in spiritual understanding.
>
> [*Discussion with Hayagriva on Auguste Comte*]

> A devotee should observe the vow of celibacy. Celibacy does not necessitate that one be absolutely free from sex life; satisfaction with one's wife is permitted also under the vow of celibacy. The best policy is to avoid sex life altogether. That is preferable. Otherwise, a devotee can get married under religious principles and live peacefully with a wife.
>
> [*Srimad-Bhagavatam* 3.27.7, purport]

> In the beginning of Krishna consciousness, one may not fully discharge the injunctions of the Lord, but because one is not resentful of this principle and works sincerely without consideration of defeat and hopelessness, he will surely be promoted to the stage of pure Krishna consciousness.
>
> [*Bhagavad-gita* 3.31, purport]

Reconciling Seemingly Contradictory Statements – How do we reconcile such seemingly contradictory statements in scripture? In another example, at one time Srila Prabhupada stated, "One must leave his family life and enter the forest after the age of fifty" and at another, "In this age of Kali-yuga, sannyasa is prohibited."

> Vedic authority says that a householder must leave home after his fiftieth year. *Pancasordvam vanam vrajet*: one must leave his family life and enter the forest after the age of fifty...In this age of Kali-yuga, taking sannyasa is prohibited because persons in this age are all *sudras* (laborers) and cannot follow the rules and regulations of sannyasa life...In

Kali-yuga the injunction is that no one should accept sannyasa. Of course, those who actually follow the rules and regulations must take sannyasa.

[*Srimad-Bhagavatam* 3.24.35, purport]

I find it very significant that both of these statements that could be taken as contradictory come from the same purport! Is it not, then, that Srila Prabhupada wants us to use our intelligence in the application of Krishna consciousness, rather than follow blindly?

Before surrendering, one is free to deliberate on this subject as far as the intelligence goes; that is the best way to accept the instruction of the Supreme Personality of Godhead.

[*Bhagavad-gita* 18.63, purport]

It is easy to see that diverse conclusions could be derived by different individuals. Conclusions can vary starting from "chanting 50 rounds is the standard and anything else is sinful" to "there are different degrees of illicit sex," on to "sex within marriage is not sinful."

My Frank Observations

I have observed that the following situations are found among couples:

- Some rare couples, having attained an elevated state of Krishna consciousness, are able to follow the highest standard and live together connected in peace and harmony.

- Some couples are able to abstain from sex because they have developed mutual resentment and dislike. They may remain together out of a sense of duty, living in strained, parallel worlds, with little sense of connection.

- Some couples are able to follow the highest standard for some time, but later concede to a lesser standard in marriage.

- Some neophyte couples are able to follow the highest standard for some time and imagine they are on an elevated spiritual platform. After a while, they may fall victim to extramarital illicit sex, pornography, and/or prostitution. Ironically, they may preach the highest principle in a fundamentalist manner.

- Some couples have one spouse who wants to follow strictly, and one who feels the need for sex. Many of these strained situations end in divorce.

- Many of our second generation, seeing a lack of affection, pervasive marital discord, and the high rate of divorce in Vaishnava and secular society, prefer to cohabit rather than marry.

The Conclusion of the Grihastha Vision Team – Our conclusion is that this a subject every couple should thoughtfully navigate with sensitivity, mutual respect, honesty, and compassion – understanding that the integrity and health of their marriage is an essential part of their spiritual life and Srila Prabhupada's mission. In establishing their values in this regard, they should seek guidance from senior grihasthas who have happy and successful marriages.

In addition, if they are unable to follow the highest standard set by Srila Prabhupada, they should find a position from which they can be peaceful and gradually progress. Sex only in marriage should be seen as platform from which couples can be encouraged to progress to the higher platforms. Sex outside of marriage is sinful and carries a reaction that is extremely crippling to family and society – divorce is devastating.

Purifying Sex Desire – One of the purposes of the grihastha ashrama, spiritual family life, is to purify sex desire. However, we don't want abstinence in marriage to be the cause of marital breakdown. We want to see that abstinence is the mature decision of both spouses. We also do not want devotees to fall prey to the conclusion that "If I can't follow the highest standard, why bother with any standards? Why chant rounds or offer food to Krishna?" Furthermore, we do not want devotees to develop a low self esteem or guilt because they cannot follow the highest standard. That situation would undermine their enthusiasm to continue in Krishna consciousness.

Consulting Senior Householders – On this subject, sannyasis, although well meaning, do not always have enough experience in household life to give the best advice. Seek guidance from senior householders in long-term, stable, happy marriages.

I have observed that devotees flourish over the long haul where the fundamentals of Krishna consciousness are stated in an uncompromising manner, tempered with encouragement and compassion. Balancing one's own reality with the highest spiritual standards is something that grihasthas ultimately will have to negotiate as a couple. In this regard, it is extremely important for grihasthas to chant their rounds sincerely, read Srila Prabhupada's books regularly, associate with devotee couples fixed in their practices of Krishna consciousness, and pray to Krishna for guidance.

Stresses on Connection and Intimacy

When I was 17, I climbed a mountain with a friend. Feeling the stress of exhaustion near the summit, I began questioning what the heck I was doing there, risking my life. I later discovered that this is a common occurrence even for experienced climbers. In a similar way:

Marriage is a journey with challenges, not a resort destination.

It is very important to internally identify and validate stressors. Failure to do so may lead you to falsely identify your marriage as the cause of distress, and thus you could mistakenly conclude that ending your marriage would end the distress.

Hot Tip – There will be challenges. There will be problems, no *ifs, ands* or *buts*. Identify problems and focus on connecting to improve and protect your marriage.

Very Hot Tip – Remember, the problem is the problem; your marriage is not the problem, it is a vehicle for resolving the problems.

Situations that Strain Connection in Marriage

Nurturing Children – In child rearing years, a woman's need for connection can be fulfilled by the reciprocation of the children. As a result, the husband may feel neglected. Take time to connect with your spouse during this period.

Stresses at Home – My wife was once being questioned by our family doctor. He asked if she was under any stress. She replied, "No, I don't think so." He asked, "Do you have any children?" She replied, "Three. One is 3 years old, one is 6 and one is 9." He said, "Lady, you're under stress!" Statistics show that marriage satisfaction tends to be at a lower level during child rearing years. This is a challenging part of the journey. Talk about your challenges with your spouse and find time to relax together alone.

Stresses at Work – Workplace stresses follow us home. Mentally, leave them in a box outside your door and pick them when you return to work. If you are unable to do this, discuss your work challenges with your spouse. Being understood and validated can help you process those emotions and move beyond them and, in the process, connect with your spouse. Unacknowledged stress can create mental filters which create undesirable behaviors such as being short tempered, grouchy, withdrawn, and picky. These are very common, and unfortunately can become ingrained in our everyday lives. We can live our values or live our filters – the responsibility is ours.

Reactive Emotional States – These states can be caused by hormonal, physiological, and chemical changes in some women and some men. Yes, ladies, even men can fall victim to hormone fluctuations! Symptoms are unexplained onset of anger, anxiety, hypersensitivity, depression, or irritability which tends to be compounded by the stressful world in which we live.

> *Irritable Male Syndrome (IMS)* – In men, Irritable Male Syndrome is further compounded by denial and thinking the problem is anywhere other than in themselves. Unfortunately, wives may become the outlet for the anger and irritability. In these situations, women, be compassionate first with yourselves, learning to deal with issues and get support if needed, and secondly, know when to insist that he, for his own benefit, make his life less stressful, get help, and treat you with the respect and compassion you deserve.

> *Women's Hormonal Issues* – In women, hormonal issues are often compounded by men's bungling responses. At these times, women are looking for empathy, for help to sort out feelings, and for someone to

lean on. It is very common for males to fail to understand the strong female need for validation. In these situations, men with good intentions try to problem solve. Men, problem solving at such times is not what she is looking for and will likely cause her to become frustrated and withdrawn, and think you are from the planet Rahu. Your spouse simply needs to connect with her feelings and feel validated. Men, if you have not grasped the concept of reflective listening, go back to Chapter 3 on communication and assimilate the section on empathic listening – hearing with your heart.

Help with Hormonal Issues – Exercise, proper diet, and avoiding certain foods can help alleviate symptoms of IMS and PMS. In some situations, counseling can help IMS. If symptoms are severe, see your doctor or health care specialist. There are medications, many of which are over the counter and natural, which can help.

Mid-Life Crisis – Life and marriage are journeys with challenges. Use your spouse as a mirror to help you see and process your challenges and help you connect with your important principles and values.

Dwelling on Differences – Continually focusing on differences can create a negative bias which will undermine your connection and could eventually cause you to rewrite your history and destroy your marriage. As described earlier, learn to understand and honor each other's differences. Doing so makes them an asset. Being resentful about differences makes them a liability. Consider that your marriage vow was intended to keep you bonded in a Krishna conscious union – not bound. In the *Bhagavad-gita*, Lord Krishna refers to the regulative principles of freedom.[4] Marriage, one of those principles, is ongoing and dynamic, not static, and it requires continual effort to maintain yours in a healthy state.

Communicate Your Needs for Connection

Sometimes one can be affected by a negative paradigm by which one thinks a Vaishnava should have no needs, what to speak of a need for affection. This is very detrimental and crippling. As we previously cited, affection is a symptom of life, and in the *shuddha-sattva* state, the condition of pure goodness, that affection maintains the devotees. Couples should respectfully and compassionately communicate what they need in order to connect affectionately in their marital relationship. This requires that couples have the loving trust to allow themselves to be vulnerable, to open their inner hearts, and to have empathy and compassion with their spouse.

Kardama Muni performed severe austerities for ten thousand years. When the Lord appeared to him, Kardama Muni expressed the need for a wife of like disposition. That certainly took courage and trust. Then the Lord revealed to Kardama Muni that coincidentally, the emperor Svayambhuva Manu was looking for a husband for his qualified daughter, Devahuti. Kardama Muni and Devahuti were then duly married. (See *Srimad-Bhagavatam* 3.21.6-27) Kardama Muni was able to communicate his need to the Lord, and the Lord responded favorably.

Conclusion

1. Intimacy is a broad subject, and couples must nurture many types of intimacy to have a healthy, loving, Krishna conscious connection.

2. Understand that the health of your marriage is important to Srila Prabhupada and his mission.

3. Live the values of alignment with Srila Prabhupada, family love and affection, mutual respect and appreciation, open and honest communication and spiritual equality / material difference.

4. Do not sweep this issue under the carpet; eventually you'll trip over it.

5. Couples should regularly practice revealing their minds and needs in confidence.

6. Think 'we', not 'me'.

7. Understand what you need in order to connect with your spouse, and understand what your spouse needs in order to connect with you.

8. Examine your paradigms (attitudes or mental maps) coming both from within ISKCON and outside of ISKCON to insure they are healthy.

9. Remember that one of the best gifts you can give your children is to show them that their parents have a warm, loving, Krishna conscious relationship.

10. Sex is a subject that couples should discuss with honesty and compassion, unless they are both on the *paramahamsa* platform, the highest stage of realization, which would make the issue irrelevant.

Well, hopefully now this "potato" is not too "hot" to handle.

About the Author

GVT

PARTHA DASA married a beautiful, kind, nurturing, and devotional girl in the last term of high school in 1971. Upon graduating, they left on a spiritual quest which culminated in taking initiation from Srila Prabhupada in 1973. Several days after taking second initiation, Partha dasa became head *pujari* for Sri Sri Radha Madana-Mohana, in Vancouver, Canada, and remained so for close to 20 years. He is a former board member and trustee for ISKCON Vancouver and has been involved with the Grihastha Vision Team since 2004. He and his wife have facilitated GVT seminars in South Africa, Ireland, England, India, Trinidad, Guyana, Brazil, Canada, and the US and have invitations from other countries. He is solemnized by the Province of British Columbia to perform legal marriages, which he does after sufficiently counseling the couple. He is certified by the Dasi-Ziyad Family Institute to administer their 'Vaishnava 108 Inventory and Premarital and Marriage Spiritual Strengths-based Relationship Program©,' along with skill building courses by various other marital therapists.

Partha dasa has three creative children and five fun grandchildren, and he is still married to the beautiful, kind, nurturing, devotional girl he met over 40 years ago. He currently resides with his wife and family in Saranagati Dhama, Canada. For recreation, he chases bears out of his garden in the summer and does telemark skiing down steep mountain slopes in the winter.

Chapter 7 Sacred Parenting: What Krishna Conscious Parents Want to Know

Sridevi dasi

with Vrnda dd

In this chapter you will learn:

✓ How to Identify the Four Parenting Styles

✓ How to Be Role Models For Your Children

✓ How to Communicate with Your Children

✓ How to Implement Rules and Routines

✓ How to see Parenting as Devotional Service

Like father like son.

Principles Highlighted in this Chapter

- Focus on Children's Welfare

- Family Love and Affection

- Exemplary Lifestyle

- Alignment with Srila Prabhupada

- Spiritual Growth and Progress

Welcome to the World of Parenting in Krishna Consciousness!

You have been selected by Lord Krishna to be the parent of a devotee child. What a great honor, privilege, and joy! As with all precious gifts, this comes with great responsibility. As Krsnanandini Dasi and Tariq Ziyad say in the preface to their parenting skills training curriculum, *Parenting for the 21st Century*:

> Family is the springboard from which we all jump, slip, slide or get pushed into life. It is a powerful social institution that is fundamental to the well-being of children and adults. Like other institutions, the family is deeply entwined with many other necessary social traditions. The first school, the first educational system in which a child will ever participate, is the family. A child's initial place for information about spirituality or religion…is the family. The first recreation center, the first place where we play…is in the family. Almost all of the important basic skills required for healthy life are initiated in the family. *A healthy well-adjusted child is more likely to make a healthy, balanced spouse, friend, neighbor or citizen of the world.*[1]

Sounds important, doesn't it! Now ask yourself, who taught you how to be a parent? Even if you have never signed up for a parenting course, you have been trained by…society? Possibly. The media? Probably. Your own parents? Inevitably.

What have you learned about parenting? Many young parents are determined NOT to repeat their parents' child-raising mistakes – yet find themselves recreating the same emotional climate and even repeating the very phrases they vowed never to say to their own children! It is possible, however, to replace the recordings that have been playing in our heads since our own childhood.

Examining our parents' parenting style can be helpful.

How were you parented?

Parenting can be classified[2] as:

- Authoritarian ("I'm the parent; my way or the highway")

- Permissive ("Whatever you want, dear")

- Authoritative ("Let me hear your needs; let's see how we can fit them in to the structure")

Barbara Coloroso, author of the parenting best-seller *Kids are Worth It: Giving Your Child the Gift of Inner Discipline*,[3] coined the term "Brick Wall" for the Authoritarian style, "Jellyfish" for the Permissive style, and "Backbone" for the Authoritative style. As she points out, a backbone gives both structure and flexibility.

A Permissive style might spring from indulgence ("Whatever you want, dear, that's what I want you to have") or from neglect ("Whatever you want, dear, I don't care").[4]

Look at the following chart[5] to see which parenting style you were raised in. What aspects of your childhood led you to identify that one?

Brick Wall (Authoritarian)	Indulgent Jellyfish (Permissive)	Neglectful Jellyfish (Permissive)	Backbone (Authoritative)
High in rules and limits	Low in rules and limits	Low in rules and limit.	Sets appropriate limits. Adjusts to time, place, and circumstance
Low in warmth and affection. Low responsiveness	High in warmth and affection. High in responsiveness	Low in warmth and affection. Low in responsiveness	High in warmth and affection. High in responsiveness
Inflexible with the rules.	Few or no rules.	Few or no rules.	Flexible with the rules.
Has the attitude of "my way or the highway"	Allows kids to do what they want. Gives in easily to their requests and demands	Allows kids to do what they want. Doesn't pay attention to their request or demands	Encourages participation from children: they always "get their say" although they may not always "get their way"
Punish rather than discipline, teach or correct. "Obedient child" lacks initiative	Little or no structure. Little or no con-se-quences to teach children right from wrong "Spoiled child"	Little or no structure. Little or no con-se-quences to teach children right from wrong "Wild child." Truancy and delinquency common	Dealings with children are marked with a balance of firmness, kindness, affection and reasonable expectations "Well-behaved, confident child"
RESULTS: Children are likely to be conscientious, obedient, and quiet, although not especially happy; more likely to be depressed or feel guilty, self-blaming. Rebel as adolescents	*RESULTS: Children are likely to be even less happy and to lack self-control, especially within the give and take of peer friendships; their inadequate emotional regulation makes them immature and impedes friendship formation*		*RESULTS: Children are likely to be successful, articulate, intelligent, happy with themselves, and generous with others; tend to be liked by teachers and peers*

What effect do these parenting styles have on child development outcomes? Researchers have conducted numerous studies that have led to several conclusions about the impact of parenting styles on children.

- **Authoritarian "Brickwall" parenting styles** generally produce children who are obedient and proficient, do well in school and other activities, are "high achievers," yet they rank lower in happiness, social competence, and self-esteem.

- **Permissive/Indulgent "Jellyfish" parenting styles** often result in children who rank low in happiness and self-regulation. They experience problems with authority and tend to perform poorly in school. These children don't learn to control their own behavior and always expect to get their way. They often end up as the "spoiled brat." They may also be involved with misconduct and drug abuse. Yet, since the world at large is not indulgent and will provide natural consequences to their actions, some of these children grow up to be emotionally secure, independent, and willing to learn from defeat.

- **Permissive/Neglectful "Jellyfish" parenting styles** produce children who rank lowest across all life domains. These children tend to lack self-control, have low self-esteem, and are less competent than their peers. Children often display contradictory behavior and are emotionally withdrawn from social situations. This disturbed attachment also impacts relationships later on in life. In adolescence, they may show patterns of truancy and delinquency.

- **Authoritative "Backbone" principled parenting styles** tend to produce children who are happy, capable, and successful.

It is extremely helpful to evaluate the impact of the parenting you received. How is it affecting the parenting you are giving to your children? Your spouse also is carrying around the recordings of how he or she was parented, which might not be with the same style as you grew up with! Remember that patterns can be changed. Balancing firmness with sensitivity for a child's emotional needs for self-expression is not easy for those of us who, as children, were rarely treated with respect or sensitivity. Conversely, setting boundaries may be difficult for someone raised without much structure. Either way, this calls for introspection and self-work.

Healthy Families

Research from Family Wellness Associates,[6] corroborated by research studies all over the world, shows that no matter the race, economic status or age, all healthy families exhibit the following three healthy skills and three healthy patterns:

> Our own upbringing has a huge impact on how we parent our children. Take time to reflect on the parenting you received and how it is affecting your interactions with your children.

Three Skills of Healthy Families

1. Healthy families **Cooperate** to get things done so that family members meet their needs. Healthy families realize that *"teamwork makes the dream work."*

2. Healthy families **Speak respectfully** to express feelings, desires and concerns.

3. Healthy families **Listen carefully** to understand.

Three Patterns found in Healthy Families

1. In healthy families **Adults are in charge**. At least one adult is providing leadership at all times.

2. In healthy families, there is **Room to be close and apart.** Each family member is free to get close to and separate from each other.

3. Healthy families **Expect to change**. Healthy families expect that they will go through changes as children grow and life events happen. Expect that change is part of the life cycle of a family and be flexible as it unfolds.

Healthy Families have a spiritual foundation and live according to principles including truthfulness, cleanliness, compassion, self-discipline, and service to others.

What are the duties of parents?

1. To help their children have a healthy sense of self

2. To teach their children right from wrong, by guiding and disciplining

3. To set good examples for their children on how to interact with others

4. To provide for the physical, emotional, social, intellectual and spiritual needs of their children

5. To create and maintain a secure family life

6. To protect their children from harm

In the *Srimad-Bhagavatam,*[7] it is stated that no one should become a mother or a father, a teacher or a leader of any kind unless they can save their dependents from a hellish life. This recognizes that parenting is a tremendous responsibility. However, if a child does not decide to actively practice Krishna consciousness when he or she grows up, you should not think that you have failed as a parent or as a devotee. Children are individual spirit souls with the same independence that we have. Ultimately, you give them the best you can, and hope and pray for the best. According to an Indian saying, "Raising children is like packing a trunk, what you put in first – comes out last!" In other words, the training you give them in the early years will always be there for them.

Being Role Models for Your Children

It is important to be aware of the impression that our behaviors are leaving on our children's minds and hearts. Children learn by following their parents. As far as possible, try to **be consistent** – children are very quick to pick up on discrepancy between our words and actions, especially during adolescence.

What does it mean to be consistent? Does it mean you have to do everything exactly the same every time, with no allowance for time, place, and circumstance? Does it mean that both parents have to have exactly the same reactions to everything? Does it mean that the grandparents can't have different house-rules from the parents? Actually, it doesn't mean those things – it means something even harder! It means having principles and values and consistently following through on them in all the changing circumstances, even when it is inconvenient for us.

As Krsnanandini Dasi says, "This is sometimes very challenging. Parents may start a routine, but as time passes they become slack or irregular." Slacking off for our short-term convenience is different from having a reason to adjust for time, place, and circumstances.

Let's look at Rohini dasi as an example. Rohini decided to try for peaceful bed-times by starting a bedtime routine at 7:00 each evening. Her son Abhay began to notice that if a friend called her to chat, the start time of the bedtime routine would get set back, so he didn't take the bedtime routine idea very seriously. He also learned that he was not as important to his mother as her friendships were.

However, there may be circumstances that justify setting aside a rule or a routine. Postponing the start time for the bedtime routine because of casual chatting with a friend is one thing; delaying the start of the bedtime routine once in a while for a very serious reason – for example because a friend has just had an accident and you need to go bring her children to your house for the night – is another thing altogether. Explaining the situation to your children helps them understand principles and values and also helps them understand how to apply the time, place, and circumstance exceptions to the rule.

To be consistent, you have to mean what you say and follow through on it. We've all seen parents who, at the end of a visit, say to their children "We're leaving now; put on your coat and shoes." The young ones barely glance up from their play. The mother stands at the door with her hand on the doorknob, chatting with the hostess, interspersing her chat with a few more exhortations to the children to get ready to go. Finally she raises her voice, and they drop their play and run to put on their shoes. On the way to the car, the mother wonders out loud: "Why do I have to raise my voice to get you to stop playing and get ready to go home?" She doesn't realize that she has trained her children that she doesn't really mean it until she raises her voice.

Often, being consistent will be very inconvenient for us as parents. It may mean having to take a restless child out of a *Bhagavatam* class that we've been looking forward to; it may mean having to cut short a supermarket trip to remove a child who is having a tantrum; it may mean having to arrange babysitting in order to run errands. Ultimately, it means that you take your role as a parent so seriously that your child's training takes priority over your own convenience.

Dayal Nitai dasa and Chaitanya dasi were members of an active youth group. As the years went by, the members of the youth group matured, married and had children. In their busy lives, the Sunday Feast was their main chance to reconnect with each other. It became common to see the former youth group members gathering as friends after *prasadam*, while their children ran wild through the temple. Dayal Nitai was concerned about the possible hazards of the steep stairs and the balcony, but he really didn't want to give up the chance to associate with his friends in order to supervise his young sons. His values were in conflict – he valued his children's safety and their enjoyment with their peers at the temple but he also valued his time with his friends and his wife's social time in their friendship group as well. To be consistent with all his values, he expressed his needs to Chaitanya dasi and negotiated some arrangements for supervision of the children, involving alternating parental duties with friendship and even paying a responsible 12 year old who had taken a baby-sitting course to take a shift with the children periodically so that both he and his wife could be together to interact with their friends. This took time and resources to organize – Dayal Nitai chose consistency with his values over his own convenience.

Sometimes, being consistent with our principles and values will require expressing our concerns and negotiating to make changes to the current situation. Allowing children to observe their parents' successful negotiations to implement their values is role-modeling at its finest!

Setting a Spiritual Example: Let your children see your personal relationship with Krishna, and help them develop their own relationship with Him. Let them see that after rising and taking bath, you go and pray to the Deity. Let them know that you pray for ability to do your daily activities for Krishna. Let them know that in your prayers you explore your mistakes and ask for His mercy and guidance. Encourage them to think of Him, offer their new possessions to Him, and bring Him some gift daily. As Uttama devi dasi says, "It's only the personal relationship that lasts; rituals can drop away if your children find no deeper meaning in them."

Careful observance of our vows, contributing to the community by our participation, tithing, supporting the Temple, offering charity to worthy recipients, and offering hospitality to guests will help our children understand Vaishnava etiquette and desired behaviors. (Incidentally, this also creates a supportive network that nurtures our children: it does take a village to raise a child.)

Honesty is the Best Policy: It is best to be honest with your children about your own shortcomings. For example, it is common when stressed to lose our temper and say things in anger or frustration, but then making amends is an absolute necessity.

You may say, "I'm sorry I lost my temper. I was a little stressed today and needed to take 'time out' myself." Or "I wasn't able to finish chanting my rounds today, so I'm going to make them up tomorrow." This kind of openness and honesty helps children learn that no one is perfect, and that it is all right to admit to our imperfections while taking steps to improve.

Your Marriage: its effect on your children

Children Are Affected by the Family's Emotional Climate – The family provides the greatest environmental impact on a growing child. Children are like sponges, and they are absorbing all that is going on around them. Even babies pick up on the emotional climate surrounding them. It is crucial that there is harmony and a good atmosphere in the home. This means putting your own relationship in order, ideally well before the children arrive. But if not done before, then at any stage it is a welcome move. If needed, ensure that you get marital education and the skills you need to make your relationship harmonious and the home peaceful.

Find a marriage mentor in your community – Talk to senior devotees with happy, stable, long-standing marriages. If necessary, locate a relationship therapist or marriage educator in our Vaishnava Family Resources Directory and learn to heal and grow. The best gift that you can give your children is having a happy marriage yourself.

Ages and Stages: child development and appropriate expectations

From Vedic times to the present, it has been noted that child development goes through stages. Srila Prabhupada mentioned the *kaumara, pauganda, kaishora* and *yauvana* stages.[8] Currently in the Western world, it is common to talk in terms of infants, toddlers, pre-schoolers, school-aged children, and teenagers. Researchers such as Piaget[9] and Erikson[10] have identified stages along the continuum of cognitive development and social development. Even though every child is unique and grows at his or her own pace (and a wise parent won't make comparisons between siblings or neighbours), still it is useful for parents to have age-appropriate expectations.

For example, children tend to think very concretely and specifically in earlier stages of life. The ability to think about abstract concepts usually does not occur until they are more than 10 years of age. A two year old child can follow one simple command at a time; if more than one command is given to her simultaneously, she will be confused. Age-appropriate instructions will save you, and her, a lot of frustration!

Here is what Srila Prabhupada says about different treatment and expectations at different ages:

> Up to five years the child is given full liberty – whatever he likes, he may do…It is said that you can give liberty to the child only for five years….And as soon as he is on the fifth year, you must be very strict on the child, on the boy, so that he may not be spoiled. Very strict. Simply engage him in proper education…And as soon as he is on the sixteenth year...the son, the boy should be treated as friend…So from sixteenth year to twenty-fifth year, higher education. And after higher education,…family life.
>
> [Lecture on *Srimad-Bhagavatam* 7.6.6-9
> – Montreal, 23 June 1968]

Srila Prabhupada's words, like a sutra, require some unpacking. What does it mean to give a child full liberty – 'whatever he likes, he may do?'

Ideally, during the first five years, the child develops trust in his caretakers, explores his environment, and builds confidence in his ability to do things independently. 'Full liberty' facilitates the development of this trust and confidence. Therefore, a parent should avoid imposing a lot of rules that restrict a child's curiosity and exploration. At this age, the child's safety is better protected by parental vigilance than by rules. For example, when two year old Madri is climbing onto the kitchen chair, loving hands need to be close by.

Children's Responsibilities at Different Ages

At a very early age, children are interested in helping with household tasks, and their self-esteem is greatly enhanced by being allowed to take appropriate responsibility. The following chart indicates the age range within which it is possible that young people could begin to learn the life-skills listed. Many parents might be surprised at the age ranges suggested, preferring to wait until the child is clearly independently capable of performing these tasks with a minimum of instruction. However, children become progressively less enthusiastic about learning these skills as they get older, because they are busy with other activities and these tasks no longer represent inclusion in the world of grown-ups. The information in this chart provides a very useful list for taking advantage of the child's initial interest and enthusiasm.

Of course, learning how to take on these responsibilities starts with a lot of parental hands-on training.

Remember: children grow at different rates and some may not be ready for specific responsibilities as early as others.

Also, please note: **no child should be expected to do all the tasks for any given age group**.

General guidelines for learning responsibilities

2 and 3 year olds can learn how to:

Put away books and toys	Brush teeth and hair	Sweep floor
Make simple food choices	Wash hands and face	Help carry in groceries
Clear own plate and take it for washing	Put dirty clothes in hamper	Hang coat on low hook
	Dress and undress with help	Become toilet trained

4 year olds can learn how to:

Help plan grocery list	Help with yard and garden chores	Share toys with friends
Help shop		Bring in the mail
Put away groceries	Help vacuum and make beds	Play in a secure area without constant supervision and attention
Help make lunch	Dust	

5 year olds can learn how to:

Help plan meals	Clean own room and make own bed	Fold and put away clean clothes
Make own simple breakfast or snack and clean up	Choose clothes and dress self	Answer the phone and make own calls
Pour own drink	Clean the sink	Pay for small item in store
Tear lettuce for salad	Wash mirrors and windows	Take out trash
Combine ingredients for simple recipe	Separate laundry into piles by color	Get an allowance and decide how to spend it

6 year olds can learn how to:

Peel veggies without adult supervision	Choose clothes appropriate for weather or special events	Bring in firewood
Use stove with adult supervision	Hang up own clothes in closet	Clean out car
		Pull weeds, rake leaves
Prepare own lunch for school	Carry own lunch money and notes to school	Clean up sink and tub after own use, hang up clean towels
Put away clean dishes		

7 year olds can learn how to:

Wash, oil and lock up bike	Write down phone messages	Sweep and wash porch or patio
Carry in grocery bags	Wash walls and floors	Water lawn
Run errands		

8 year olds can learn how to:		
Mop floors	Help shop for his/her own clothes	Vacuum rugs
Help arrange furniture		Paint fence or shelves
Start to read recipes and cook simple family meals	Sew on buttons	Supervise younger siblings for short periods
	Write a simple letter	

9 year olds can learn how to:		
Change own sheets	Schedule homework and practice times	Wait on guests
Operate washer and dryer		Sew, knit, and use a sewing machine
	Plan his/her own parties	

10 year olds can learn how to:		
Use comparative shopping and buy groceries	Manage money, use a bank	Keep track of his/her own appointments and remind parents of transportation needs
	Take city bus on his/her own	
Earn money by doing chores for the neighbours	Wash the car	
	Pack a suitcase	

11 and 12 year olds can learn how to:		
Mow the lawn	Take a paper route	Join organizations, attend meetings, and take on assignments
Clean oven and stove	Check and add oil to car	
Prepare more complicated meals	Read a tire gauge and inflate car tires	Become a leader in an organization

Teenagers can learn how to:		
Earn money	Open and maintain a checking account	Stay home alone while parents are away on a trip
Use the family car with permission and proper license		
	Use a credit card (with parental permission)	Decide with parents on a curfew

The teen years are the time for young people to discover who they are as individuals separate from their family. Sometimes this looks like rebellion against their family. Barbara Coloroso[11] has some pertinent points on this topic. One of her main points is that children should be helped to think for themselves from an early age. If they can make their own decisions independent of you, they will also be able to make their own decisions independent of their teenage peers. If they are independently thoughtful by the time they are a teenager, who are they going to be rebelling against? There is no point rebelling against their own decisions!

Read and study scientific information about being a teenager. Read about the physiological and mental changes that adolescence brings. That will give you insight into the very real challenges accompanying the growth and development of your teen.

Let your children experience that there are consequences for every choice they make. Sometimes, we're tempted to shield them from the natural consequences of their choices. Try to avoid shielding them, because it can interfere tremendously with their development and their mature learning.

Practice the communication technique of Reflective Listening/Respectful Speaking with your adolescent. A common complaint from teenagers is that parents don't listen to them. This invaluable communication technique will ensure that your teenagers feel heard and respected.

Communicating with Your Children

How many of us have seen the five-year-old chatterbox grow into the fifteen-year-old who answers questions with barely a monosyllable? The Dasi-Ziyad Family Institute teaches that "Communication is key in parenting." Their handbook strongly suggests that parents "practice the **Reflective Listening/Respectful Speaking** communication technique every day, in all relationships, but especially with children, including teens."

Even if we are familiar with reflective listening techniques (see chapter 3) and regularly use those skills with adults, we might not have extended this to our children. Krsnanandini Dasi suggests that we overcome any awkwardness by practicing with a child, and points out that the child we practice with does not have to be our own child.

Let's look at a few examples of a parent using Reflective Listening with a child.

Reflective Listening with a pre-schooler:

Five-year-old Bala Gopala announces that he is bored.

His mother bites back her first comment, which would have been a judgemental "How can you be bored? You have more toys than a toy store" or a directive "If you can't think of what to do, I suggest you tidy up your room." She remembers that she is trying to be respectful with Reflective Listening, so she gives him her full attention and says "I'm hearing that you feel bored, that nothing really interests you at this moment."

"That's right, I feel real bored!" says Bala Gopala, coming right up to his mom for a snuggle.

"Hmmm, bored!" says his mom, bending her head to connect with his.

They remain like this for a few heartbeats, then Bala Gopala breaks away saying "I'm gonna build a fort in the back yard!" and races off.

Reflective Listening with a school-aged child:

Eight-year-old Abhideya is in the third grade at school. In the evening, her father asks her "How was school today?"

"Okay, I guess," she says.

Her father almost says, "That's good, dear; mine too" but remembers that he wanted to try Reflective Listening, so he says "Sounds like nothing was too bad and nothing was super good…"

"Yeah," says Abhideya, looking up to check if her dad is still interested. "Actually, there was one thing I didn't like." She paused.

"Something you didn't like?" her father echoes, still giving her his full attention and succeeding in holding back his inclination to give platitudinal advice about life being like that.

"Yeah, today in math drills. Tomorrow is going to be awful. Today I got the whole page right in 48 seconds, so tomorrow I'm supposed to do it in 45 seconds. I don't think my hand will move that fast! I think today was the fastest I can go!"

Her father feels his eyebrows rise along with his urge to call the teacher, but he remembers that he is Reflective Listening, so he says, "I'm hearing that you are really concerned about the math drill tomorrow."

Abhideya doesn't say anything right away; she just looks thoughtful. After a minute she says "Tomorrow, before we start math, I'm going to ask my teacher what I'm supposed to do if my hand just won't write any faster. Thanks, Pita! I feel a lot better now!"

Reflective Listening with a teenager:

Fourteen-year-old Kaishori's high school is near her mother's office, so Kaishori walks over to the office after school and gets a ride home with her mother. Often Kaishori is a little prickly, and her mom, Yashoda-mata dasi, is rather probing. Usually their conversations during the drive home leave both of them feeling irritated.

Yashodamata is pretty sure that she has learned about Reflective Listening too late to help her relationship with Kaishori, but she decides she has nothing to lose so she gives it a try.

"How was your day?" she asks, as she always does.

"Whatever," says Kaishori as usual.

Yashodamata resists her urge to ask specific questions like "Did you get your essay back yet?" or "Do you think you did well on your algebra exam?" Instead, Yashodamata just says, "Not a really super day." She glances over at Kaishori, but Kaishori isn't looking at her.

Kaishori does notice the glance, however, and after a minute she says with a little more animation, "Yeah, not the best day ever."

Yashodamata tries, "Sounds like it wasn't your favorite day," feeling like an idiot for echoing, but impressed that the conversation hasn't yet become prickly.

In fact, Kaishori turns toward her slightly and says, "Yeah, Kenzie said she'd have lunch with me, but then she went and sat with some kids from her old school."

Yashodamata feels her heart breaking for her daughter, but manages to say just "Sounds like that wasn't a great experience."

"It sure wasn't!" says Kaishori. "I didn't know what to do – whether I should just join all of them anyway, or send Kenzie a text asking what was going on, or what."

"Sounds like you felt hurt and confused," says Yashodamata, hoping Kaishori wouldn't feel judged by that statement.

"That's for sure," Kaishori replies. "It makes me wonder about Kenzie. Maybe she just doesn't have what it takes to be a friend. I'm just gonna watch for a while and see what she's really like."

Yashodamata glances over to meet her daughter's gaze, and realizes it had been days since they had looked each other directly in the eye.

Yashodamata can't wait to share this experience with her parenting group. She feels really motivated to get good at this amazing skill.

Most of us didn't grow up seeing good communication skills in action every day, so we can use some support as we learn these new skills. The Dasi-Ziyad Family Institute recommends books such as *How to Talk So Kids Will Listen & Listen So Kids Will Talk* by Adele Faber and Elaine Mazlich. As Krsnanandini Dasi says, "Parents with strong communication skills and a real commitment to their children's growth and development generally maintain strong relationships with their children."

Hints about Rules and Routines

Young children love routines. Routines give them a chance to predict what is going to happen next, and to be right! Here are some hints and guidelines from the Dasi-Ziyad Family Institute:

Guidelines for establishing routines:

- Make sure the routine is practical and that it accomplishes the purpose.

- Make sure your children know what is expected of them. Family meetings are an excellent time to talk about family routines.

- Let children help make the routines when possible.

    Sample routine: To put my children to bed by 9:00 p.m., we will have a routine that begins at 8:30, get a half glass of warm milk, herbal tea or water, brush teeth, put on pajamas, and read a bedtime story.

You may find that routines are sufficient to keep family activities moving smoothly. However, there may be times when you feel a need to implement a few rules. If so, here are some hints and guidelines, again from the Dasi-Ziyad Family Institute:

Guidelines for making family or household rules:

- Keep the rule simple.

- Be consistent and clear about the consequences of breaking a rule.

- Make sure you have a family meeting to explain the rule.

- Don't have too many rules. (It's OK to remind them of the rules – post the rules in a prominent place, like on the refrigerator).

    Sample rules:

    □ No television after 8:00 p.m. for children age 10 and under.

    □ Older children wash their clothes on the weekend.

- Family must have dinner together unless someone is out of town or working.

Consequences are what happens when rules, routines, and family courtesies are not followed. They should be discussed with the children so that they are aware of what will happen. Make the consequences relate to the behavior. For example, when your child refuses to wear a jacket to the park and it turns cold, let him experience the chill. When Mitra spills juice on the floor, give her a cloth to clean it up. If Abhimanyu doesn't want to pick up his toys after you've reminded him, take the toys away for a while (depending on his age, for a few hours or a few days).

Effective Discipline

What is the difference between discipline and punishment? Discipline is related to the word 'disciple'; discipline is proactive, focused on learning for the future: "Here's what to do next time." Punishment is reactive, focused on what was done wrong in the past. Punishment is arbitrary and aims to hurt or deprive the child. Discipline is not arbitrary; it is related to the offense because the aim is restitution and becoming aware of the natural outcomes of misbehavior. Punishment only addresses the misbehavior itself; discipline looks for the feelings and needs that caused the behavior.

Enforcing punishment has a different effect from applying discipline. Because punishment ignores the feelings and dignity of the child, punishment inspires anger, resentment, and even rebellion as the child feels misunderstood. Discipline, however, preserves dignity and mutual respect, and motivates the child to do better next time. After a discipline session, the parent and child feel good about each other and the relationship. The parent is teaching self-control by explaining the reasons for certain behavior, and power struggles decrease as the needs of both parent and child are addressed. However, when punishment is applied, the control is external, the relationship suffers, and power struggles will increase because only the needs of the parent have been met.

Often when misbehavior has occurred, the parent feels angry. When as parents we are angry, we are much more likely to punish than to discipline. Punishing might make us feel better for a short time – but it is not a very effective training tool, and we might actually feel guilty about the punishment when our anger has dissipated. Rarely do we need to discipline immediately. Giving ourselves a time-out to calm down and decide how to handle the situation respectfully can actually save time in the long run.

How can we tell if we are disciplining or punishing? Here are some scenarios; for each scenario we have provided a possible discipline response and a possible punishment response. See if you can tell which is which.

Scenario 1: Ramananda Raya and the Bike Helmet

Ten-year-old Ramananda Raya has gone for a bike ride without his helmet – again.

> Ramananda Raya's father tells him that because he didn't wear his helmet, he won't be allowed to accompany his classmates on an upcoming camping trip.

> **OR**

> Ramananda Raya's father asks him why he doesn't want to wear the helmet. Ramananda Raya explains that he doesn't think about the helmet till he gets out to the bike, and then he doesn't want to go back up to his room to get the helmet. His father says that wearing the helmet while biking is non-negotiable to protect Ramananda from head injury, and if he can't ride safely, the bike will have to be put away for a week. He then asks Ramananda Raya what could be different that would help him put on the helmet.

Which one is punishment? Which one is discipline? Why?

Scenario 2: Taraka's Curfew

Twelve-year-old Taraka was allowed to play outside with her friend until 8 o'clock. She comes home at 8:30, but shows her parents that her watch says 8:00.

> Taraka's parents tell her how much they worried about where she was from 8 till 8:30, and how they had gone looking for her and were almost ready to ask the police to help find her. They also tell her that when they were kids, they had tried that same trick of setting their watches back to try to get more play time. Then they ask her what she would do if she could go back in time and do it over again.

> **OR**

> Taraka's parents take her watch away, telling her she doesn't need it if she can't use it properly. They also tell her that because she lied to them, she won't be allowed to use the computer for a month, not even for homework.

Which one is punishment? Which one is discipline? Why?

Scenario 3: Chandravali and the Vase

In a dramatically bad mood, fifteen-year-old Chandravali breaks her mother's favorite flower vase which was just the right size for the family altar.

Chandravali's mother tells Chandravali that she expects a sincere apology and a new vase the same size.

OR

Chandravali's mother tells Chandravali that Chandravali is incurably clumsy and will be grounded for a week and not given her allowance for a month.

Which one is punishment? Which one is discipline? Why?

Scenario 4: Sunanda and the Family Car

Seventeen-year-old Sunanda was allowed to use the family car to take his friends to a Pandava Sena event with the strict understanding that he would have the car home in time for his father to drive his mother to a medical appointment for which she has been waiting six months. He returns the car half an hour after the agreed time to find his parents have gone to the appointment in a taxi.

> Sunanda's parents shout at him about how irresponsible he is and how he will never be allowed to borrow the car again. For the next few days, every time they see him they narrow their eyes, purse their lips and shake their heads.

> **OR**

> Sunanda's parents ask him why he was late and why he didn't call. They tell him how worried they were about his safety and how torn they were about deciding whether to postpone the long-awaited appointment with the specialist. They tell him they expect him to pay for the taxi, and they ask him to explain to them why they should trust him with the car the next time.

Which one is punishment? Which one is discipline? Why?

With Ramananda Raya and his bike helmet, forbidding the camping trip has nothing to do with the bike helmet – the parent is using hurt and deprivation to get the child's attention, but this is likely to cause resentment because of the injustice. Even taking the bike away does not increase the chances of him later using the helmet if he has some objection to wearing it – however it may be a necessary short term consequence to keep Ramananda Raya safe, rather than a punishment. For the long term, we need to find out why he doesn't wear the helmet and then help him take steps to overcome his objection. This would be an instance of **looking for the feelings and needs that caused the behavior.** Knowing that his bike will be put away for a while if he doesn't wear the helmet, Ramananda Raya is motivated to explore his own objections and find a way around them. In this case, he just didn't want to have to go back to his room to get the helmet. He suggests that the bike helmet could be stored closer to his bike, and asks his father to install a hook just inside the garage. Since he came up with the solution, he feels some ownership of it, which is better than if his father said "I know what, I'll hang your helmet in the garage for you so you don't have to go back to your room." However, in a different situation, the objection might not have been about the ease of getting the helmet – it might be about the helmet itself. It might not fit well anymore, or his friends might have told him it was 'geeky.' Only patient listening will discover the underlying cause of the non-compliant behavior.

Taraka's manipulation of time to get more playtime is something that needs discussion, but taking away her watch and computer privileges is punishment which is counterproductive to a successful resolution.

> The greatest gift you can give your child is high self-worth. Fostering a sense of deep value and high self-esteem in your child will be an invaluable gift that will last a life-time.

In Chandravali's case, an apology and a new vase is what an adult friend would give us if the friend caused a similar accident. Therefore we can tell that it is not punishment to expect the same of Chandravali.

Shouting and scowling at Sunanda won't actually help him understand the point of view of the people he let down. **Seeking to understand** what was happening for him, asking for **restitution** and talking about **'next time'** are aspects of discipline.

In addition to handling misbehavior in a loving, teaching way, there are some things that parents can do to prevent misbehavior from happening in the first place. One important proactive measure is to make sure our children are very clear about the behavior we expect of them. When they can say it back to us, we know they at least heard it clearly. This investment of time is worthwhile to help protect their self-esteem, so they don't have to learn everything by being caught doing it wrong.

Krishna Conscious Education

A devotee education is ideal, if you live in a community that has an organized devotee school. If you have to send children to public school, they will need a well developed spiritual after-school or Sunday school program, so that they can learn verses, act in plays depicting the pastimes of the Lord, chant *japa* and kirtan, and learn to play instruments for devotional music. However, whether the school is a Krishna conscious school, a public school or a private school, the home is the biggest influence. Therefore it is important that the home environment gives lots of opportunities for Krishna conscious activities.

Some parents, seeing the challenges posed by public school, have opted to come together and home-school their children, with excellent results. Home-schooling is recognized by many educational jurisdictions, and many school districts will provide resources for support.

> Read a bedtime story as part of your evening ritual. As well as helping transition to sleep-time, the bedtime story builds your children's vocabulary and provides topics for discussion. Even after they can read for themselves, continue the bedtime story with books about 2 years ahead of their own reading level.

Another important resource for home-schooling is Aruddha devi dasi's book *Homeschooling Krishna's Children*,[12] which provides guidance for creating a curriculum based on *Srimad-Bhagavatam* without sacrificing academic subjects, starting a homeschooling co-op in your community, making 'life' your children's classroom, and navigating the college admissions process.

Effects of Media and Communication Technology

A serious challenge today is the relentless voice of the media. The average child today is 'connected' for over 40 hours a week in a way that defines their sense of the 'real' world. Srila Prabhupada once said that reading mundane books (and we could include other media as well) is like sitting on a freshly painted park bench: you walk away with a little bit of the paint sticking to you! But, unfortunately, you can't always see it. In other words, how the media contaminates us is not always immediately visible, but it has long term effects. So be very watchful and intentional in this area.

Although it may be desirable that the family and children have no interaction with such possibly harmful influences, this is often not possible. Rather than trying to completely shield family members from the outside world, it is usually preferable to teach and equip them to make the right choices. To do this, one must be a worthy example to one's partner and children.

Avoid having a TV in the house; alternatively, watch Krishna conscious movies and documentaries. If you do watch TV or go on the internet, set guidelines and standards regarding such as aspects as the type of program, when to watch, and with whom. Planned watching of programs that are consistent with Krishna conscious values and the family's personal development is better than random channel surfing or internet browsing.

Thirty years ago, an effective child safety awareness program asked parents: "Do you know **where your children are** right now?" The updated version could well be: "Do you know **what your children are watching** right now?"

Avoid using the media as an electronic babysitter. If your children watch TV or use the internet, do it together and discuss the content as you go.

Heart & Soul Connection

Special Situations

Single parents, blended families with step-children, adoptive families, and families of children with special needs may have some special challenges in parenting that may need extra help. Please connect with experienced professionals who can assist you.

Parenting = Devotional Service

Parenting devotee children *is* devotional service, and no one need be apologetic about attending to their children's needs at the expense of other services. Srila Prabhupada wrote:

> It is the duty of the parents to see that the children are growing luxuriantly not only materially, but spiritually also. So spiritual training should be given from the very beginning.
>
> [Letter to Dayananda and Nandarani,
> 24 August 1968]

> For you, child worship is more important than Deity worship...These children are given to us by Krishna, they are Vaishnavas [devotees] and we must be very careful to protect them. These are not ordinary children, they are Vaikuntha children, and we are very fortunate we can give them chance to advance further in Krishna consciousness. That is very great responsibility, do not neglect it or be confused. Your duty is very clear.
>
> [Letter to Arundhati, 30 July 1972]

Taking Care of Yourself

When we are constantly working and taking care of others, we are using up our stores of energy. Thus, our batteries need to be recharged. Both you and your loved ones will benefit by your taking good care of yourself. One of the common reasons women especially are prone to depression and stress is the misconception that taking time for oneself is "selfish" and therefore unthinkable. Not so! Every individual belongs to Krishna and devotional service to Him means we take good care of His property – our bodies and minds and hearts – so we can serve Him well!

Priyanka, mother of two small children, has been feeling irritable and stressed of late. She complains of feeling tired all the time, lacks energy and is unenthusiastic about any new ideas that her husband Prashant suggests. When her doctor found that she was putting on weight, in spite of the fact that she was constantly on the move with her two small kids, her doctor ordered bloodwork. It turned out that her thyroid was underactive.

Once she started medication, Priyanka began feeling much better within weeks. At the end of six months, she was back to her old self. She needs to take her medication regularly, but now she no longer is tired or stressed and her weight is back to normal.

If you have been on an airplane recently, you will have noticed that before takeoff, the attendants give a little demonstration on how to use the oxygen masks. They also make a statement that applies as much to parenting as it does to air travel – put on your own 'oxygen mask' first! You can't be helpful if you aren't breathing. Take care of yourself!

KEEP YOUR SADHANA STRONG! Do not forget to practice an attitude of gratitude for all your blessings! Pray, develop good reading habits of transcendental literatures – Srila Prabhupada's books – especially daily reading of *Bhagavad-gita As It Is*, attend at least one worship service at home or the Temple, and maintain loving relationships with others!

Let me quote Prahlada Maharaja:

> O my Lord, I am very much afraid of the materialistic way of life… And…the remedies which I undertook were more dangerous than the disease itself. So I drift from one point to another, birth after birth, and I pray to You therefore to give me a shelter at Your lotus feet.

> [*Srimad-Bhagavatam* 1:19:20, purport]

There is a reason your children have come to you. They, like you, have come to the point, after many lifetimes, of seeking the shelter found in spiritual life. As parents, you are performing the service of protecting and teaching little Vaishnavas. Thus you are exactly the kind of servant that Krishna is talking about when He tells Arjuna:

> For one who explains this supreme secret to the devotees, pure devotional service is guaranteed, and at the end he will come back to Me. There is no servant in this world more dear to Me than he, nor will there ever be one more dear.

> [*Bhagavad-gita* 18.68 – 69]

Therefore, in closing, I repeat the words that opened this chapter on Sacred Parenting: You have been selected by Lord Krishna to be the parent of a devotee child. What a great honor, privilege, and joy!

About the Author

GVT

SRIDEVI DASI (Dr. Lakshmi Dajak, MD, PhD), an initiated disciple of His Holiness Candramauli Swami since 2006, likes to offer a variety of services for devotees. She enjoys leading kirtan, giving class, cooking and sewing for the Deities, serving the *gurukula* children, entertaining devotees with original songs and dramas, and serving and assisting her husband and family. She has an MD in Pediatrics and Newborn Care, and practiced as a doctor in India before getting deeply interested in helping people using mental health therapy. She also has a PhD in Marriage and Family Therapy and now offers help as a Relationship Specialist. She is married to Nanda Suta dasa, disciple of His Holiness Niranjana Swami, and lives at peaceful New Talavan, Mississippi, USA, an ISKCON farm community. She has one daughter who is studying Architecture in India. She offers premarital education and therapy to individuals, couples, and families in USA and all over the world through Skype, an online video messaging service.

Chapter 8 Marriage Under Attack: Dealing with Serious Conflict, Separation, and Divorce

Krsnanandini devi dasi

In this chapter you will learn:

- ✓ How to Honor Your Marriage Commitment in Hard Times
- ✓ How to Prevent Serious Difficulties
- ✓ How to Recognize Abuse
- ✓ How to Have Hope
- ✓ Practical, Spiritual Approaches to Dealing with Persistent Conflict

Half Baked © David Musterer

Principles Highlighted in this Chapter

- Positive and Realistic Vision
- Mutual Respect and Appreciation
- Commitment and Dedication
- Open and Honest Communication

Introduction

When your body is in serious pain, maybe the last thing you want to hear is that "you are not this body." Similarly, when you encounter serious problems and challenges in your marriage, reminders about tolerance, forbearance, forgiveness, and so on may not seem so appealing. Yet these very reminders will not only help you to move beyond the challenges, but to do so while still making spiritual progress toward your chosen goal. This chapter will provide spiritual perspectives and tools to assist you when you navigate troubled waters in your marriage.

Here are some key words for householders dealing with serious conflict, separation, and divorce:

- Patience
- Prayer
- Surrender
- Faith
- Creativity
- Appreciation
- Forgiveness
- Commitment

> Arguments (or disagreements) are a natural part of any relationship, but cruelty is not. Above all, happily married partners see each other as allies, not as adversaries.
>
> – Bill Doherty, PhD, Department of Family Social Science, University of Minnesota

Case Study

A Marriage Starting Out with High Hopes – The following case study will be referred to as we discuss various aspects of serious conflict, separation, and divorce:

> After getting off to a hopeful and enthusiastic start seven years ago, the marriage of Subhadra and her husband Parampara (not their real names) appears to be going sour. Subsequent to their grihastha fire sacrifice wedding ceremony, and during the first four years of their union,

they lived within walking distance of a temple and participated almost daily in temple worship and other devotional activities. Two children were born in those first four years.

Then Parampara lost his job, and they moved in with Subhadra's mother, who although sympathetic to Krishna devotees, is a Christian lady whose lifestyle is different from her daughter's and who lives more than 20 miles from the nearest temple. Parampara appears to battle with depression and lately has been spending hours at the computer, sometimes even viewing pornography. Subhadra has found a part time job and is feeling that her marriage is falling apart. Arguments between Parampara and Subhadra have accelerated in intensity and frequency. Sometimes she questions if she actually made the right choice seven years ago.

How many marriages face similar challenges, even though they started out with hope and promise? Most of us never expect our marriages to fall apart or end in divorce.

So, You Had a Different Idea About How Your Marriage Would Be...

Is Divorce Normal? Let's face it; marriage is work – especially when the support so necessary to maintain any healthy family or marriage is practically nonexistent. Sometimes, despite every effort you've made, it seems it would be best to separate or divorce. So many divorces occur in America and other parts of the world that many people claim divorce is normal. But as Diane Sollee, the Founder/Director of SmartMarriages.com, points out, "Saying 'divorce is normal' is like saying polio is normal, and let's focus all our resources on building a better iron lung and not spend money to develop a vaccine."

Some people equate failed marriages with broken spiritual vows – For devotees of the Lord who have taken vows to maintain spiritual standards of morality, perhaps making those vows before the Deity and the community of Vaishnavas, a failed marriage involves more than just a marriage breaking up – it may trigger a feeling of failure in one's spiritual life.

Like Subhadra in our case study, you may have reached a point in your marriage where you think you can no longer tolerate your spouse's behavior. The love, and perhaps also the respect, has evaporated like smoke being pulled up by an exhaust fan. You feel it may be best to consider divorce. Yet, as a serious practitioner of spiritual life, you recognize that you made a commitment that you really want to honor. You struggle with doubt and confusion about the vows you made; your spouse doesn't make it any easier because his/her behavior is not improving. In fact, there are definitely behaviors in your spouse (or yourself) that signal trouble for your relationship. But you aren't sure if these things are beyond repair or should simply be tolerated.

Danger Signs In a Marriage

Subhadra knew that she was in the throes of multiple threats to her marriage. She began to research to see if others had some suggestions for her. Here's a list of some danger signs she identified through her research. As she listed them, Subhadra could see that her relationship with Parampara had some of these danger signs.

1. **Your spouse has a history of abuse.** In his or her past, there are definite incidences of verbal, emotional, or physical abuse. Past baggage and dysfunctional behavior can really cloud current relationships. One or more family members will likely benefit from counseling to help recover from the past experiences.

2. **You tend to give more than you receive in the relationship; you perceive that your relationship is not reciprocal.** Your marriage may have diminished into a one-sided relationship where you seem to do all the forgiving, all the compromising, and all the surrender. To Subhadra in our case study, this seems true. Her husband's depression has robbed him of his motivation. His sadhana, his devotional practice, has weakened considerably. To her, it feels like she is carrying practically the entire weight of keeping the family together.

3. **You think your spouse has a lot of potential but it just never seems to manifest, even after much time spent together.** In fact, you often ask yourself some version of this question: "What did I think I saw in him (or her) that would contribute to creating a healthy union?"

4. **You fear "being yourself" around your spouse**. It's easier to behave in ways that he or she prefers, rather than to just be yourself and express your true feelings or tastes.

5. **People you love and trust advise you that your spouse is not acting in your best interests.** Trusted friends and family are really worried about you in this marriage.

6. **Your spouse habitually tells lies and is generally devious.** It has gotten to the point that when your spouse speaks, you don't know whether to believe what he or she says.

7. **You and your spouse have little or no fun together**. In our case study, Subhadra and Parampara could not recall the last time they did something fun together.

8. **Your relationship lacks affectionate dealings.** The children don't see their parents acting with gentleness, respect, or genuine affection. One day, Subhadra's son asked her if daddy still loved her.

9. **You and your spouse ignore or avoid problems, or even avoid each other.** Whenever Subhadra would bring up a troublesome subject, Parampara would withdraw.

10. **You or your spouse, or both of you, act selfishly.** The mood is "how can you, my spouse, make me happy," rather than "how can we serve each other" or "how can I make my spouse happy." Activities are done for one's own bodily or mental satisfaction.

11. **You and your spouse have recurring arguments that never seem to get resolved**. Spats or confrontations happen over and over and are rarely resolved. While most couples may have disagreements, having repeated sarcastic, disrespectful altercations is a very real indication of a seriously conflicted relationship.

12. **You and your spouse have experienced a general breakdown in communications.** In our case study, the lack of communication skills is obvious; neither knows how to speak respectfully or listen reflectively, and conflicts are not handled with the goal of win-win results.

13. **There is evidence of inappropriate behavior with members of opposite sex or actual infidelity.** In a healthy marriage, a respectful, principled marriage, there are important guidelines for proximity or closeness to the opposite sex. Your spouse should be aware, approving, and generally present when you deal with the opposite sex.

14. **You or your spouse, or both, have threatened to separate or divorce.** Even in anger, one should strictly avoid bringing "the D-word" into discussions. Once introduced, it can be a frustrated end to every argument or disappointment, and eventually become a sad, self-fulfilling prophecy.

Although the signs above indicate danger, all is not lost if they are present in your relationship. Becoming aware of the problem is the first step to making changes. Counseling or marriage education will be needed, however, especially when you have more than one of the danger signs in your relationship.

Marriage and Divorce Statistics

In today's world, characterized by Kali Yuga's qualities of quarrel and hypocrisy, we should not be surprised to find challenges to healthy marriages everywhere. In the Vaishnava community we are certainly not immune to these challenges. Consider these statistics from the secular North American community:

- Over 50% of new marriages and 65% of second marriages fail.

- More than 200,000 new marriages each year end before the couple's second anniversary.

- 57% of divorces are due to poor communication skills and poor conflict-resolution skills.

- Less than 20% of marriages receive sufficient premarital preparation.

The Costs of Divorce – Divorce wreaks havoc on families and devastates children. It's very difficult to calculate the amount of pain and destruction to a family. Divorce is for life, and, particularly if children are involved, divorce can be a long-time frustrating and costly experience. Negotiations, visitations, money matters, courts, and lawyers can be a part of your life forever. In fact, there are often so many unwanted dealings with your former spouse. And if he or she is absent from the children's life, the negative effects of father/mother absence are now well documented. Look at what research is showing:

- 63% of youth who commit suicide come from fatherless homes.

- 85% of children exhibiting behavioral disorders come from fatherless homes, as do 80% of incarcerated youth, 90% of homeless runaways, 85% of children exhibiting behavioral disorders, 70% of juveniles in state run institutions and 71% of high school dropouts. Additionally, young children growing up without fathers are 10 times more likely to be living in extreme poverty.

What To Do About Challenges to your Marriage

Marriage Education and Counseling – Marriage intervention, through healthy marriage relationship skill-building education, can be quite effective in dealing with the danger signs cited above. Seeking the help of trained, experienced, mature, and committed Marriage and Family Educators or counselors, who are themselves dedicated to practicing spiritual life, will go a long way to provide you and your spouse with relationship skills and tools to strengthen your marriage.

The Grihastha Vision Team's website at VaisnavaFamilyResources.org is one place to go for resources. If both you and your spouse want to strengthen your marriage and are willing to follow through with the work required, then there is every reason to believe, by the grace of Guru and Gauranga, that your marriage can be salvaged and more than that, enriched.

Even if only one of you is willing to do things differently or try other ways to interact, there is still hope. There are many relationship skills such as Reflective Listening/Respectful Speaking, Turning Complaints into Requests, Win-Win Problem-Solving and similar tools for empowering you with the ability to communicate and resolve conflict on a more effective and spiritual level. (See Chapter 3: "Let's Talk About It: Open and Honest Communication")

Grihastha Vision Team Members – Members of the Grihastha Vision Team (GVT) are marriage and family educators, marriage and family counselors, and social workers. Most are experienced in providing marriage and family education through workshops, magazine articles, books, and direct couple services.

Some of the couples who come to the GVT to participate in marriage education or counseling sessions are considering divorce, and some may just have a marriage that's neutral – not vibrant but not painful. We've seen couples in our marriage-education classes completely revitalize their marriages, whether on the brink of divorce or not.

Seeing great improvement in marriages gone sour is not unique to GVT marriage and family educators. In the words of Dennis Stoica, President of the California Healthy Marriage Coalition, "Couples on the brink of divorce recapture intimacy, trust and caring, and those with an OK marriage can take it up to levels of satisfaction they never experienced before." And Mr. Stoica should know: his coalition has provided marriage education to more than 20,000 people! Marriage education can help! You can find a list of devotee marriage educators on the Grihastha Vision Team's website VaisnavaFamilyResources.org.

The following comments[1] from Visakha devi dasi, a senior disciple of Srila Prabhupada, offer a thoughtful perspective on how to view difficulties in marriage:

> Marriage is difficult; once that fact is accepted, it no longer matters. Sometimes, because of false ego, there may be tremendous conflict and disagreement between husband and wife, but if, in this darkness, their mutual commitment to their relationship prevails, that commitment can carry their relationship beyond its troubles to greater intimacy. When quitting is not an option and is not justified, the alternative - sooner or later - is overcoming the difficulty. Difficulties are inevitable, but overcoming them - not quitting - is optional and requires our discipline, courage and wisdom. Our reward is to again resonate, to grow in kindness, in trust and in trustworthiness. Problems and conflict are not an opportunity to quit but to move forward, to become unstuck. As Krishna is mystical, so non-negotiable commitment to His service is also mystical because, by His grace, we can deal with a problem when we take responsibility for it. When the Lord sends us a test, He simultaneously gives us the ability to pass that test if we so desire. 'The Lord is so kind to His devotee that when severely testing him the Lord gives him the necessary strength to be tolerant and to continue to remain a glorious devotee.'[2]

Recently my own marriage was seriously tested by the return home of one of our children and two grandchildren. Shortly thereafter, my mother also came to live with us. This happened, interestingly enough, at a time when my husband and I were looking forward to having more space in our home and less responsibility because our older children were either off to college or living on their own and we had the just the two youngest children still at home. Our adult child and my mother were dealing with depression and other personal challenges. To say that this time was stressful would be a great understatement.

My husband and I strained to serve them, our younger children, and each other, all the while maintaining equilibrium in our home and fulfilling many other duties. We've closed the door to divorce in our marriage. So we had to work hard utilizing prayer, time, mutual respect, regular family meetings, reflective listening techniques (with the younger children too), and some dedicated help from our other adult children. These tools and extended family support enabled my husband and me to draw deeply upon our friendship and commitment to one another while dealing with this crisis together.

All of us grew from this experience; both my mother and our daughter had an opportunity to heal in a spiritual and nurturing environment, although they sometimes resisted the help and we had to show "tough" love. This was a very rough patch in our marriage, but my husband and I developed a greater appreciation for one another and realized even more how much we relied on each other's support and understanding.

Importance of Marriage Education

Let's return to the case study of Subhadra and Parampara to get more of a sense of how marriage education can help a troubled marriage.

> Acting on a suggestion of a devotee friend, Subhadra contacted a couple who provided marriage and family education. When she told them her story, they agreed to work with Subhadra and Parampara in a systematic way for approximately 12 hours. Subhadra and Parampara worked with the Marriage/Family Educators to identify their own values and to set financial, family, and personal goals. The experienced Marriage/Family Educators taught them communication and conflict resolution skills, and requested that they practice these skills daily.

> Subhadra and Parampara were encouraged to brainstorm ideas for transforming their situation. They learned how to really listen to each other without judging, criticizing, or shaming each other. They were given symbolic Reflective Listening Tools and urged to practice and re-practice using these communication tools. The couple also was urged to clarify the spiritual principles that were the foundation of their relationship and to recognize how important it was for them to practice these principles.

> Through marriage education, Subhadra and Parampara were able to reestablish and recommit to a new vision and a practical plan for cooperating together for their mutual growth. They set goals for themselves and their family and agreed to hold weekly family meetings. They learned to look out for behaviors that de-energize couples and invite marital difficulties.

Four Disempowering Behaviors that Threaten a Marriage

According to social scientist John Gottman, there are Four Horsemen of Marital Apocalypse.[3] (In this context, "marital apocalypse" refers to a complete destruction or devastation of your marriage.) In other words, there are four behaviors that should be avoided if you want a satisfactory marriage and one that is pleasing to the Lord:

1. **Criticism** – "Why did you pick that stupid-looking shirt?" You or your spouse or both, constantly point out the faults in the other's behavior, clothing, or choices.

2. **Contempt** – "You are disgusting." "You're fat now." Your words or gestures (or those of your spouse) frequently express a strong feeling of hostility, implying that the other person is somehow unworthy, inferior or not deserving of respect.

3. **Defensiveness** – "Yeah? You're always talking about me. What about what you did?"

4. **Stonewalling** – shutting down – associated with high physiological arousal and efforts to self-soothe with thoughts like "I can't believe she's saying this!" Stonewalling means to stall or delay – especially by refusing to answer questions or to cooperate. This behavior is extremely damaging for both the one who withdraws and the recipient of such neglect. It is often used to control.

The thing to remember here is that none of these behaviours result in healthy interactions or good feelings – none of these behaviours get you the results you want!

> Subhadra realized that she had been contemptuous and critical of her husband for a long time. Parampara could acknowledge that he was always feeling himself on the defensive and definitely used stonewalling to avoid Subhadra's "attacks." By opening their eyes to how much these negative behaviours were sabotaging their marriage, both agreed to use their reflective listening tools and practice win-win problem solving. For example, they brainstormed some creative ways for Parampara to find employment and use his talent to earn more income for their family. Instead of blaming each other, they focused on some of the external challenges that were affecting their marriage.

We Can Learn to Counter These Four Disempowering Behaviors

Tendency to Criticize and Speak Contemptuously – To counteract the tendency to criticize and speak contemptuously, try to pray daily for the ability to act as instructed by Sri Chaitanya Mahaprabhu:

> *Trnad api sunicena, taror api sahisnuna,*
> *amanina amanadeya, kirtaniya sada hari*

> One should be more tolerant than a tree and more humble than a blade of grass and ready to offer all respect to others… In such a state of mind, one can chant the holy name constantly.[4]

Having the privilege to call upon the holy name of Krishna means that we call on the greatest help because the name is non-different from the Supreme Loving Lord Himself. Thus we get so many of the benefits that come from the presence of the Lord: peace, guidance, and, gradually, a mature intelligence. If you can, chant together with your spouse at least once a day.

Practice doing just one thing different when you talk to your spouse. For example, speak in a softer tone of voice, lowering the volume of your voice when you might normally speak loudly.

Study and practice the six kinds of loving exchanges between Vaishnavas: offering *prasada* (sanctified food), accepting *prasada*, revealing one's mind in confidence, listening confidentially, offering gifts in charity, and accepting gifts.

Check yourself from time to time and make sure you are engaging in these loving exchanges. Doing so will prevent you from taking your spouse for granted.

Tendency to be Defensive and "Stonewall" Your Partner – To counteract the horsemen of Defensiveness and Stonewalling, practice the communication skills of Reflective Listening/Respectful Speaking and "Finding the Pony." There are specific guidelines to using these techniques that will help you avoid defensiveness and stonewalling.

"Finding the Pony" Helps to Ease Conflict

As mentioned above, one of the techniques Subhadra and Parampara learned was to "Find the Pony," and they tried to use this technique when they were frustrated or confused with one another. You can do the same. When you and your spouse are having difficulty connecting or understanding one another, "Finding the Pony" is a technique that is quite effective in opening the door to healthier communication.

Here's the background story: Two brothers, in eager anticipation of Christmas gifts and fun, go obediently to bed the night before Christmas. As soon as day breaks, they bolt down the stairs to look under the Christmas tree only to find nothing but a big pile of horse manure under the tree! One brother, in utter frustration and disappointment, trudges sadly back upstairs. The other brother runs around with excitement, shouting "Where's the pony? Because where there is manure, there's a pony!"

Finding the Pony is about acknowledging the need of the other person (spouse or spouse-to-be) without blaming yourself for some inability or inadequacy. Find what the actual need of the person is without making yourself the victim. It's about finding the gift that hides under the "mess," the gift that would allow you to connect with your spouse.

Here are some examples:

- You come home late from work and your spouse complains that you are "never home on time." Finding the Pony: It seems that your spouse really desires your association! Now that you've found the pony in your spouse's seeming criticism, acknowledge aloud that your spouse would appreciate specific time set aside for you as a couple or family.

- One spouse becomes upset because the other allowed their teen-ager to do some unapproved behavior. Finding the Pony: It seems that your spouse takes parenting very seriously. Tell your spouse that you realize he or she wants some agreed-upon parenting rules, and offer a time to discuss it.

- One spouse returns home to find the house cluttered and messy and complains angrily about it. (He or she probably had a rough day at work, too.) Finding the Pony: Realize that this person values order and calmness. Acknowledge aloud that your spouse wants to see order and calmness when he or she comes home after a long, tiring day.

- One spouse spends too much money – the other feels very frustrated and gets angry. Finding the Pony: Acknowledge that your spouse cares about having enough money to pay the bills or save up for a rainy day.

- Husband accuses wife of watching too much TV and neglecting her spiritual life. Finding the Pony: It seems the husband cares about his wife's spiritual progress.

- Husband often goes out with bachelor friends, and his wife complains that he does it all the time. Finding The Pony: Husband acknowledges that he understands that she would like for them to spend more time together. He could also say that he knows she wants to feel special to him.

- Wife calls her husband a hypocrite because he is having difficulty giving up a bad habit, when it doesn't appear to her to be so hard to break that habit. Finding the Pony: Husband recognizes that his wife wants or needs some honest dialogue about the situation so that together the couple can help each other progress in spiritual life.

When you feel that someone is dumping on you, "find the pony" by looking for the "positive" that they are trying to get to, the positive underneath the negative.

Serious Abuse

The four disempowering behaviors mentioned above, Criticism, Contempt, Defensiveness and Stonewalling, can be resolved through marriage enrichment and education.

The symptoms listed below, however, are far more intense and can indicate actual physical, verbal, or emotional abuse. They require more specific and serious intervention:

- Your spouse never takes responsibility for his or her actions and blames you instead.

- You relinquish more and more of the social or spiritual standards you have previously established in order to acknowledge the demands of your spouse and to keep "peace" in your relationship.

- Your spouse regularly ridicules your opinions or ideas, makes repeated rude remarks about your appearance, threatens you physically, calls you names, or embarrasses you in public.

- You are regularly subjected to unwarranted jealousy, false allegations of infidelity, and controlling behavior, even to the point of isolation from family and friends.

- Your partner or spouse often makes excuses for his or her cruel or unkind actions. Frequently, he or she will apologize without really changing their conduct. There is inconsistency between your spouse's promises and his or her conduct.

- You are subjected to physical actions such as hitting, biting, and kicking, or emotional cruelty such as neglect, or withdrawal of affection, or verbal abuse including your spouse subjecting you to name-calling, isolation, habitual criticism, sarcasm, humiliation, or his or her limiting your access to financial and/or family resources.

Separation until the Problem is Cleared Up – Please note that the above behaviors must be *consistent* or *regular* in order to be labeled abuse. For example, if your spouse calls you a name once or twice, later apologizes, and name-calling is not a problem you have to deal with on a regular basis, this is probably not abuse; rather it likely indicates the need for improved relationship skills.

If you are really experiencing serious abuse, however, it may signal a time to separate from your spouse until he or she gets needed help and while you receive support. No matter what, the intention to honor your marriage vows should be a priority. That is, even though you separate because of severe abuse, try to remain chaste to your vows and prayerful that Lord Krishna, who desires that we have peaceful marriages, will work in your life and that of your spouse to transform your relationship.

Srila Prabhupada on Commitment and Dedication

When internal and external pressures push on a marriage, there can be serious conflict, explosive tension, or extreme unhappiness; you may inevitably think about separation or divorce. Reflect on what Srila Prabhupada, the Founder-*Acharya* of the International Society for Krishna Consciousness, instructed his followers about the marriage commitment:

> Yes. Wife and husband, once combined, that is for life. There is no question of separation, in all circumstances. Either in distress or in happiness, there is no question of separation.
>
> [Arrival Address – London, 11 September 1969]

> The two marriages recommended by you may be performed at that time as well, but only after having sufficiently counselled the respective devotees. This marriage business should not be taken as a farce, but is a very serious matter. Recently so many couples have been cast adrift by the waves of maya's influence. That is hard to check, but still the devotees must realize the responsibilities of household life. And there is no question of separation. Too much this has been happening, and I am very much displeased. So, if they are promising not to separate under any circumstances, but to work cooperatively in the service of the Lord, then my sanction is there for their marriage, and my blessings as well. Otherwise, not.
>
> [Letter to Bhagavan, 7 July 1971]

Srila Prabhupada wanted couples to be counseled *before they were married*. He already knew what we have come to appreciate – marriage education is preventative. Not only does marriage education prepare couples by equipping them with healthy relationship skills and tools while strengthening the spiritual foundation on which strong marriages are built, but marriage education also helps couples to have realistic expectations. For example, when children are born, marriages experience another new set of stresses and strains, and there are things couples can and should do to nurture their marriages at this time. The case study presented at the beginning of this chapter shows how marriage education teaches people to resolve conflict effectively in ways that cause both parties to win.

We can see from the strong statements above that Srila Prabhupada was firm about avoiding separation and divorce. He was very compassionate however, and allowed that if extreme circumstances warranted, couples could separate.

> It is not that a chaste woman should be like a slave while her husband is *naradhama*, the lowest of men. Although the duties of a woman are different from those of a man, a chaste woman is not meant to serve a fallen husband. If her husband is fallen, it is recommended that she give up his association. Giving up the association of her husband does not mean, however, that a woman should marry again and thus indulge in prostitution. If a chaste woman unfortunately marries a husband who is fallen, she should live separately from him. Similarly, a husband can separate himself from a woman who is not chaste according to the description of the shastra.

[*Srimad-Bhagavatam* 7.11.28, purport]

If you do decide to separate or as a very last resort, divorce, do so after much prayer and reflection and with the intention to allow Lord Sri Krishna, in His own sweet time, to heal your marriage. Thus try to remain chaste, fulfilling your duties with patience and surrender. You will do well to get the services of a mature, trained Vaishnava to assist you with the separation and help you make goals for the future.

When is divorce something for a serious spiritual practitioner to consider?

Our International Society for Krishna Consciousness promotes kindness and compassion even to animals, so we should understand that this means a zero tolerance for physical abuse to our spouse. Unfortunately, abuse can occur when people are not very advanced in spiritual life or when they have some serious issues about power, control, and self-worth. If you are the victim of physical abuse or extreme emotional abuse, then, in consultation with mature, concerned devotees, divorce can be considered.

In ancient times, there were communities that supported marriage; fathers, brothers, and sons offered powerful protection to their female relatives; and there was a general societal demand and requirement for responsible, accountable behavior on the part of those who, as husbands, were supposed to be protectors and caregivers.

Because these social and moral restraints are no longer in place and because of extreme circumstances, sometimes a sincere devotee may have to get a divorce. By now, you are well aware that such a decision should not be made whimsically or just because a couple goes through difficult times. If you've done everything you can do, if your life is in danger, if you have allowed some time to see if your marriage can be saved, then please don't see divorce as failure of your spiritual life. Just endeavor to keep chanting the holy names every day and following the regulative principles, and surely Krishna's grace will cover you.

Protect Your Marriage through Open and Honest Communication

One of the Twelve Principles for Successful Krishna Conscious Family Life is "open and honest communication," a proactive approach that will prevent many relationship challenges. With this in mind, we want to share some guidelines for dealing with marital problems that might arise from our involvement in technology, computers, the internet, cell phones, and online social networks.

Safeguards to Assist Your Marriage – Just as a security system in a home offers some protection, there are many safeguards you can put in place to assist your marriage by preventing problems. Taking into account the ability of modern technology to provide isolated or secret connections, couples who want to have peaceful marriages would be wise to have agreements about cell phones, the internet, and online social network activities. What is there to hide in a marriage whose goal is to please the Supreme Lord? Such sincerity and openness create confidence and goodwill, and offer protection in a world full of maya's temptations.

Behaviors to Develop Trust – One key element in a strong, healthy marriage is trust. To be trusted, one must be trustworthy, and to be trustworthy, one has to be *open and honest*. When activities and connections with others are in the open, it's less likely that illicit activities will take place. Here are some recommendations for open and honest dealings between husband and wife regarding cell phone and internet usage:

- Give each other full access to your cellular phones and E-mail accounts, including passwords

- Give your spouse access to passwords and user names to online social networks such as Facebook, MySpace, and Twitter

- Identify your marital status openly on any social network in which you participate

- Say positive things about your spouse on these public networks and seek ways to include him/her in all your dealings with the opposite sex

- Conduct phone conversations with members of the opposite sex in the open and with the awareness of your spouse

- Pornography is a serious breach of trust, and often, because of its addictive nature, help is required to disentangle from this particularly dangerous form of maya

- Remember that every situation is an opportunity to become more Krishna conscious and to help someone else to do so

Five Basic Responses to Conflict

Conflicts can escalate or de-escalate depending on the skills and the commitment of the spouses. Knowledge of the five different ways people tend to respond to conflict can help. While we may use different styles in different situations, each person generally has a tendency to use one predominant style. It is important to understand the styles people use to handle conflict. As you will see below, each style is appropriate at some time and place, but not all styles are effective in maintaining mutually satisfying relationships. Learning healthy and effective ways to manage conflict is one of the keys to successful marriage.

The five basic styles[5] of dealing with conflict are as follows:

1. **Competition** is a confrontational style which results in a "winner" and a "loser." Generally, those who are highly competitive tend to use this style of conflict resolution because they value being "right" over being "loved" (and so frequently confuse approval with love). Sometimes, this style of conflict resolution is appropriate. For example, in an emergency situation such as when a child may be about to stick a metal utensil in an electrical outlet, it is best to grab the child before he or she is electrocuted. There is no time for discussion – you just have to win that one! Competition may also be the best style to use when an important principle is more important than a relationship.

2. **Avoidance** does not resolve conflicts. Since wisdom dictates that we pick our battles, avoidance can be appropriate when time is limited and resolving a conflict is not that important. Just as turtles pull their heads into their shells, ostriches bury their heads in the sand, or a rabbit closes his eyes when faced with danger, individuals who are fearful or uncomfortable with conflict will almost always choose avoidance. However, when we use avoidance as a primary conflict resolution style, someone usually gets hurt, and more than likely the problem will resurface at a later date, often having become worse in the meantime.

3. **Accommodation** is related to avoidance, but includes one person giving in to the other person's demands. Accommodation can be useful if we see the other person's needs as greater than our own and feel that self-sacrifice will be good for the relationship. However, people who always accommodate will frequently enable inappropriate behavior and/or harbor resentment.

4. **Compromise** involves giving something to get something. Negotiators most often use this style. Compromise is valuable when there is limited time to explore options. After a short term compromise, people frequently become angry, feeling that they gave too much or that a more collaborative solution could have been found.

5. **Collaboration** is a "win-win" approach to conflict and produces the most satisfactory and long-term resolutions. Collaboration usually takes more time than other conflict response styles mentioned above. It's useful when both the task or issue *and* the relationships between two people are important. Couples can learn to collaborate to find solutions through creative brainstorming. When they both agree on a solution through collaboration, they will both be more satisfied with the solution.

> The couple from our case study, Subhadra and Parampara, with the help of their Marriage Educators, identified their preferred styles and admitted that those past conflict styles were not working. Before, Subhadra used Competition and Confrontation as her primary method of dealing with problems while Parampara resorted to Avoidance. During their marriage education sessions, they were coached how to collaborate and develop strategies for win-win problem solving.

Take a moment to reflect. Which of the above ways is your default style? Which do you think is best for a healthy marriage? Identifying your default conflict response style is the first step in choosing more effective solutions.

Further Points for Dealing with Conflict

The following points are useful to keep in mind for dealing with all types of conflict, from mild differences of opinion to serious tensions:

- **Try to see all differences or conflicts as an opportunity for growth.** Try to see challenging times as Krishna's arrangement for you to grow spiritually and to fine-tune your devotional skills. Endeavor to develop patience and to surrender the frustrations.

> *matra sparsas tu kaunteya*
> *sitosna-sukha-duhka-dah*
> *agamapayino'nityas*
> *tams titiksasva bharata*

> O son of Kunti, (Arjuna) the non permanent appearance of happiness and distress and their disappearance in due course, are like the appearance and disappearance of winter and summer seasons. They arise from sense perception, O scion of Bharata, and one must learn to tolerate them without being disturbed.

> [*Bhagavad-gita* 2:14]

> To serve one's family members with Krishna conscious love and devotion is the religious principle of the grihastha, and one should not deviate from one's prescribed duty.

- **Pray to be able to forgive and be forgiven.** "The material world is full of embarrassing and irritating situations. Unless one is inclined to be very much forgiving, he will be infected by a vindictive mentality, which spoils one's spiritual consciousness." (*Srimad-Bhagavatam* 11.3.24, purport)

- **Remember how you were attentive to your appearance, your language, and your behavior in the beginning of your relationship.** Sometimes people neglect their appearance, forget to be courteous and sweet, and take their spouses for granted. Pay attention to your cleanliness, your neatness, your thoughtfulness, and your kindness *throughout your marriage.*

- **Focus on your *same or similar* interests vs. *different* positions.** What do you both want? For example, you may constantly fight over in-law issues. What would be a healthy way you'd like to deal with your in-laws? How would your spouse want to do it? List both your ideas. Then see how you can both be satisfied or agree. You may be surprised to find that you both want the same result; the tension comes because you have different ways of accomplishing this result.

- **Don't take all conflicts personally; separate people from problems.** Stress is a given in today's world. Realize that your spouse and you are confronting pressures – societal, economic, or familial – that may sometimes be overwhelming. Human nature means that this stress may spill over into intimate family dealings. Learn the important communication and conflict resolution skills and *practice them daily.*

- **Separate people from their behavior or actions.** Say, "I don't like your behavior," rather than "I don't like you."

Remember that perception is relative. People perceive things from unique angles of vision. Try to put yourself in the other person's shoes.

Cultural Differences Must be Taken into Account

Culture plays a role in many relationship breakdowns. We know of a couple comprised of an African-American lady and a gentleman from Pakistan. They appeared to be hard-working, conscientious people who married without the assistance of premarital counselling. Because there were some very serious cultural expectations regarding the role of male and female, and because they had no strong spiritual foundation when they married, marital discord surfaced in their relationship, and they eventually divorced after less than seven years of marriage.

On the other hand, another couple from two diverse backgrounds learned how to respect and even appreciate their different cultural upbringings. The husband was from South Africa and the wife was from Europe – yet they learned early on to emphasize spiritual principles in their marriage and to allow each other the space to honor their respective cultures. They raised their children to appreciate the rich variety of cultural resources they could draw on from each of their parents. This couple learned to communicate and identify the values that were important to them.

What is significant is that the first couple allowed their different cultural backgrounds to cause division between them while the second couple took into account their cultural differences but used these to enhance their relationship, rather than diminish it.

Some Closing Thoughts

Before you get married, you should, as Srila Prabhupada instructed, get premarital counseling or education. Once you have made your marriage vows, try to do everything you possibly can to have a healthy, vital, committed marriage. Qualities such as selfishness, unkindness, impatience, contempt, ingratitude, and lethargy or laziness are warning signs of trouble in any relationship, whereas gratitude, forgiveness, kindness, and a pleasant service attitude are characteristics that encourage healthy relationships. For devotees, marriage is a service or duty we accept in accordance with instructions from the scriptures. A marriage done well should make us better servants of the Lord – as should a marriage in which we've sincerely given our best efforts.

When you have done everything you can to keep your marriage intact, yet it appears that you cannot avoid separation from your spouse, prayerfully try to set up some agreed upon method of interacting with your spouse that will be the least unhealthy. Sometimes you may consider separating with the idea to get back together after some healing work has been done. Again, seek assistance from a mature, trained, and dedicated Vaishnava or a mentor couple in this process. If you are concerned about confidentiality, make a simple request of the mentor couple to insure that what you share is confidential.

In this material world, conflict exists. As Vaishnavas endeavouring to please the Lord, we pray for healthy relationship skills and the Vaishnava qualities of forgiveness, patience, tolerance, appreciation, and commitment in order to successfully navigate through the grihastha ashrama, demonstrating that even through difficulties, we maintain our faith and trust in the Lord's instructions. By making an earnest effort to try the techniques suggested in this chapter, all the while adhering to guidelines from sadhu, shastra, and guru, may we be blessed by our dearest friend, Lord Krishna, so that our conflicts are reduced to challenges, and the challenges will serve to strengthen the loving bonds of our marriages.

About the Author

KRSNANANDINI DEVI DASI is a minister, a Certified Family Life Educator (CFLE), President of the Grihastha Vision Team, Co-Director of the Dasi-Ziyad Family Institute (www.dzfi.org), and dedicated mother of ten children. Raised in a Christian family, Krsnanandini studied Islam, Mormonism and other religions to appreciate the underlying unity in all the world's religions. On Radhastami, September 12, 1972, she was initiated into Vaishnavism by Srila Prabhupada in Dallas, Texas, and has been a practitioner of bhakti-yoga, the yoga of love and devotion, since that time.

Along with her husband, Tariq Saleem Ziyad, she has served hundreds of individuals and couples, providing them with healthy relationship skills. She and Tariq have designed and/or implemented several workshops and curricula relating to marriage, family and youth, including the Young Pioneer Project, the S.E.L.F. Healthy Relationship Course, From Couple to Couple Mentor Couple Training, *Parenting for the 21st Century*, a 16 lesson curriculum for a variety of parents – and more. Krsnanandini devi dasi appeared in the documentary "SpiritWorks" and in "ONE: The Movie" with Deepak Chopra, Ram Dass, Thich Nhat Hanh, and Bhakti Tirtha Swami. She is author of the "Booklet of 8's: A Concise Guide to Spiritual Living", *How to Raise Your Children Spiritually,* the *First Book of Hare Krishna Puzzles, Quizzes and Riddles,* and contributor to the book *All-In-One Marriage Prep: 75 Experts Share Tips & Wisdom to Help You Get Ready Now.* She and her husband travel around the globe spreading the message that with a serious spiritual foundation, people can learn skills and make commitments to create and maintain healthy, happy relationships and marriages.

Chapter 9 A Balanced and Sustainable Marriage

Karnamrita dasa

Steadiness in one's own position is declared to be actual piety, whereas deviation from one's position is considered impiety. In this way the two are definitely ascertained.

[*Srimad-Bhagavatam* 11.21.2]

In this chapter you will learn:

✓ The Importance of Having Balance in One's Body, Mind and Activities

✓ How Balance Supports Your Spiritual Life

✓ How to Determine Your Life Priorities and Act Accordingly

" Why don't we use common sense?"

Principles Highlighted in this Chapter

• Regulated, Balanced, and Exemplary Lifestyle

The Human Condition

If we were animals, then our life would be a simple matter to balance. In fact, for animals, 'being balanced' is hardly a concern, as this is their instinctual nature, guidance from the Lord in their heart. Everything is already worked out. Their basic necessities, such as what to eat and how to sleep, mate and defend, are built into their instincts. Animals are just trying to survive and to avoid being killed by predators.

For human beings, it is a different matter. Human life is like being on parole from prison. It is a beginning step in understanding the soul's perilous condition living in the world and having to take birth after birth in the material prison house. Therefore, as humans, we have special facilities of advanced reasoning, intelligence, and sense of right and wrong, along with the ability to love and give selflessly. In addition we have a natural curiosity about our place in the world, about the meaning of suffering, and about our purpose for being here.

Other than our special human facilities, we share identical basic concerns with the animals: to keep the body alive through eating, sleeping, and fearing (or defending), and to create progeny. Those of us who are fortunate to have taken up the path of Krishna consciousness need to take care of our animal propensities in ways that are favorable to our spiritual life. This is one of the foundations of balance.

The Important Things in Life

In *First Things First*,[1] Stephen Covey relates an experience shared by a colleague:

> I attended a seminar once where the instructor was lecturing on time. At one point he said, "Okay, it's time for a quiz." He reached under the table and pulled out a wide-mouth gallon jar. He set it on the table next to a platter with some fist-sized rocks on it. "How many of those rocks do you think we can get in the jar?" he asked.
>
> After we made our guess, he said, "Okay, let's find out." He set one rock in the jar…then another…then another. I don't remember how many he got in, but he got the jar full. Then he asked, "Is that jar full?"
>
> Everybody looked at the rocks and said "Yes."
>
> Then he said "Ahhh." He reached under the table and pulled out a bucket of gravel. Then he dumped some gravel in and shook the jar and the gravel went in all the little spaces left by the big rocks. Then he grinned and said once more, "Is the jar full?"

By this time we were on to him. "Probably not," we said.

"Good!" he replied. And he reached under the table and brought out a bucket of sand. He started dumping the sand in and it went in all the little spaces left by the rocks and the gravel. Once more he looked at us and said, "Is the jar full?" "No!" we all roared.

He said, "Good!" and he grabbed a pitcher of water and began to pour it in. He got something like a quart of water in that jar. Then he said, "Well, what's the point?"

Somebody said, "Well, there are gaps, and if you really work at it, you can always fit more into your life."

"No," he said, "that's not the point. The point is this: if you hadn't put these big rocks in first, would you ever have gotten any of them in?"

What Are Your "Rocks"? Your "Sand"?

Setting Your Priorities – Keeping in mind this story, what do you think are your personal and marriage "rocks" or "sand"? You have to do that for yourself; I can't tell you what they should be. In my experience, there isn't an exact black-and-white one-size-fits-all "formula." The abovementioned book by Stephen Covey could be a resource for you, since it dedicates 15 chapters to a detailed process for getting a good look at your own priorities and then making time for them in your life. The key, says Covey "is not to prioritize your schedule, but to schedule your priorities."[2]

That's just what Gauranga dasa did. Here's how it happened:

Several years ago, as part of a professional development seminar at work, Gauranga was asked to fill in a values pyramid. He placed his Krishna conscious practices right near the top.

The presenter then told the group that they need to give their top three values sufficient time in their life in order to feel happy. "If you don't live your values," the presenter said, "life feels out of balance; you just don't feel happy."

Gauranga dasa realized he actually gave very little time to his spiritual life, in spite of valuing it so highly. "It was a 180° turn-around realization," he says now. "I started chanting all my japa again, I took a job closer to the temple, and I started attending and participating more."

The result? Scheduling his priorities put them back in balance with the rest of his life.

How do you discover what your priorities really are? As with any good project management, Covey's process has you 'begin with the end in mind' – the end, in this case, being your deathbed for this lifetime.

Maybe you could take a minute now to think about what will really matter to you as this lifetime is ending. Typically, people on their deathbed don't think about the money they made or the honors they received – they usually remember their regrets concerning relationships and what they didn't do but should have. I hope you will stop and think about the things you consider really indispensible in your life, and how to keep them in place!

Take a minute to write down two or three things that you consider most important, that give your life meaning.

1.

2.

3.

Now that you've thought about the things you really want to include in your life, ask yourself: What percentage of your time are you spending on those priorities?

You can see from this exercise that balance is NOT about becoming faster and more expert at juggling all the balls you have in the air, so that you can add more! At its core, balance comes from personal decisions about *which* balls you want to keep in the air.

Even more important than achieving an acceptable level of segregated activities is the practice of integration: integrity in all your activities, leading to the accomplishment of one goal, your life's mission.

Introspection

While the human condition is similar, every person is unique. Even for one individual, priorities may be different at various stages in his or her life. For instance, a young couple with small children will have a different type of balance from a retired person with grown-up children. There is just no substitute for personal introspection in understanding how to be balanced, integrated individuals, couples, and families. Healthy, balanced individuals greatly facilitate healthy, balanced marriages.

Introspection requires the humility to see the less-than-ideal parts of ourselves and accept that we have to change. Change is hard work, and it can seem easier to remain the same. In the face of the naked truth of our conditioned nature, we may try to ignore or repress the parts we don't like.

Srila Prabhupada compared chanting Hare Krishna to making ghee, the clarified butter used for cooking and ceremonies. Ghee is made by boiling butter. Gradually, the milk solids or impurities rise to the surface, and one has to remove them. Otherwise they burn and spoil the ghee.

Chanting the holy name cleanses our heart and helps us be aware of our own "impurities" bubbling to the surface. These unwanted habits of thinking and acting – called *anartha*s in Sanskrit – can be gradually removed. Chanting and associating with advanced devotees are two especially powerful processes for cleansing our heart.

Anartha-nivrittti, or retiring our unwanted habits of thinking, is one of the stages described by Rupa Goswami[3] on our journey to *prema*, or love of Krishna. Many devotees struggle with this stage because of other priorities or lack of good examples. However, in my experience, when we understand the importance of introspection in this stage, we can give it necessary time and energy. Since we all do what we consider important, we will be more motivated to seek out advanced and mature devotees and to make intense prayers for our spiritual progress.

Balanced Body

The Sanskrit word *atma* can refer to body, mind, or soul in different contexts. Thus, it should be no surprise that for our marriages to be peaceful, balanced, and conducive for our spiritual advancement, we need to address all three of these aspects of our life.

Although our soul is "who we really are" in an eternal sense, we have to act in this world with the help of the body. Vaishnava scriptures give us many practices that help to keep our body image in perspective. For example, we mark our body with *tilaka,* sacred clay, to designate it as a temple meant for spiritual practice. Therefore we must respect the body and take care of it, as part of our service to Guru and Krishna.

Sometimes new devotees, acknowledging that we are "not the body," think it is spiritual to neglect their physical necessities. This same concept can lead devotees to treat others harshly and without compassion. Sickness or frailness of body could be erroneously equated with laziness or being 'in maya,' or in illusion. However, spiritual knowledge and compassion for the soul should include compassion for the physical suffering of ourselves, our family, and other living entities.

Balanced Mind

Discussing a balanced mind could perhaps fill a whole book, but for this chapter, let me quote the *Bhagavad-gita*:

> One must deliver himself with the help of his mind, and not degrade himself. The mind is the friend of the conditioned soul, and his enemy as well.
>
> [*Bhagavad-gita* 6.5]

As Srila Prabhupada describes in many places, the purpose of the yoga system is to make the mind our friend by using it to remember the Lord, instead of allowing it to be our enemy by contemplation of material sense enjoyment, lust, or attachment to temporary material things.

Are there any parts of your life that you feel anxious about or on "overload" with? If so, these are red flags to examine. Anxiety, sadness, and depression provide internal feedback letting you know that you need to make important changes. If your depression is prolonged, you might need professional help to work through the issues.

We have the very enlightening verse, also from the *Bhagavad-gita*:

> And satisfaction, simplicity, gravity, self-control and purification of one's existence are the austerities of the mind.

[Bhagavad-gita 17.16]

This verse gives us several clues on how to make our mind our friend. The more we contemplate sense objects, the more we lose peace. Without peace, there can be no happiness (*Bhagavad-gita* 2.66). However, we become satisfied by engaging in devotional service, chanting the holy names, and working according to our nature while offering our work as service to Krishna.

Fuel for the Body, Mind and Soul

As devotees, our task is to find out how to meet the demands of the body and mind in a regulated way that is compatible with our sadhana.

> He who is regulated in his habits of **eating, sleeping**, recreation and work can mitigate all material pains by practicing the yoga system. [emphasis added]

[Bhagavad-gita 6.17]

The basic necessities of the body are proper food, water, air, activity and rest. Proper food for devotees is *prasadam,* lacto-vegetarian foods with no trace of meat, fish or eggs, prepared with love and offered to Krishna.[4] These foods are sattvic; in other words, they have the energy or quality of goodness.

> Foods dear to those in the mode of goodness increase the duration of life, purify one's existence and give strength, health, happiness and satisfaction. Such foods are juicy, fatty, wholesome, and pleasing to the heart.

[Bhagavad-gita 17.8]

The quantity of *prasadam* we honor by eating depends on our age and how much energy we are using. Overeating is not considered good for a devotee. However, insufficient eating is not advisable either. Though the six Goswamis, disciples of Lord Chaitanya, hardly ate or slept, this was a symptom, not the source, of their spirituality. Just eating less or sleeping less doesn't, in itself, bring spiritual progress. We have to be tuned in to our body to understand what it requires, and then eat, drink, and sleep accordingly. Therefore, we shouldn't be artificial about our bodily necessities, but eat and sleep according to our need, in the mood of keeping our body healthy for service.

In our youth we don't usually worry about obtaining our basic necessities, but as we acquire increased responsibilities and need to juggle more things, we become confronted with the reality that we can't do everything; we have to choose between many options. After becoming a devotee, this continues even more as now we add our spiritual practices and regulations to the mix. If we attend many devotional functions where abundant rich *prasadam* is served, we may have to be very careful to not overdo it. Additionally, as many of us increase in age, we are required to eat more simply and be more conscious of our eating for health reasons. For example, my wife has a weak constitution, so when she attends any functions she has to either bring her own *prasadam* or make sure there are food preparations that conform to her diet.

Not Excessive Attachment or Renunciation – In a very broad sense, a sustainable or balanced life for a spiritually practicing married couple means avoiding both excessive attachment on the one hand, and repulsion, or artificial renunciation, on the other.

Attachment is excessive when it overshadows remembrance of the spiritual purpose of life. The symptoms of excessive attachment are overindulgence in sense gratification or material pursuits regardless of the negative consequences. Enjoyment of the senses is compared to salt – a little is required for happiness, but not too much.

Repulsion or aversion toward material things can initially be a cover-up of material attachments, either overtly or unconsciously, due to immaturity or denial. Artificial renunciation may result in hiding one's attachments in the name of being renounced, yet secretly indulging in them, or accepting some austerity for which one is unsuited, or denying oneself something one likes or needs in a way that can't be maintained. Material attachment and aversion are different sides of the same coin, and both are meant to be retired through the purification of bhakti and experiencing the higher taste of devotional practices.

We must "do the needful" to maintain our existence, our family, and our spiritual practices for the long haul. In other words, we have to be intelligent to understand what is required for continuing our spiritual practices for our whole life, noting our changing body and mind, and making adjustments accordingly. What was once easy to do in our youth, or before a debilitating illness, may become troublesome, even counterproductive to meet our requirements for health and steady spiritual practice. My wife requires nine hours of sleep and a quiet atmosphere for rest, and has to arrange her life to facilitate that – otherwise she will become ill. Her main priority is her spiritual practices and she sees that her physical necessities are a requirement for health, service, and sadhana. She has stated that the limitations of her body have been a great teacher regarding depending on Krishna and not being fanatical. Some devotees require more facilities to be peaceful, others, less. The main purpose for being balanced in our habits is to help us be peaceful and better able to remember, love, and serve Radha-Krishna, our gurus, and the devotees.

Keeping Spiritual Practices Strong – While counseling couples, my wife and I often find that beyond the reason the couple gave for seeking help, the fact is revealed that the spiritual practices of one or both persons have been compromised, thus adding to the intensity of the conflict. Personal sadhana and shared devotional activities are essential for the long term health of the relationship. Therefore, a big challenge for many couples is to avoid being caught up in crisis mode, and instead to see their divine life as crucial to their all-around wellbeing. If they can understand that sadhana is not extra, but primary, then they can integrate their spiritual and material activities: for example, they can plan their vacation time around a spiritual event like a *japa* or kirtan retreat, or a major festival like Janmastami or Govardhana-puja, or travel to some holy place on pilgrimage.

Don't be a "Shooting Star"

We used to call devotees who artificially took on too many devotional activities, or who renounced the world prematurely, "shooting stars." They did a great deal of service – often important service – but later "crashed and burned" by not under-standing their level of spiritual advancement and their material desires. Avoiding extremes is what a spiritually and materially sustainable lifestyle is all about. It means finding our place and working from there, making gradual spiritual advancement by awakening our love for Krishna, and becoming naturally detached from whatever doesn't foster this.

Giving our Marriage Relationship Proper Care

Our marriage should also be seen as having an existence of its own, which needs to be given time and care. As individuals need proper care to live and prosper, so does a relationship. Relationships will not survive on automatic pilot, but need "TLC" (Tender Loving Care) and re-adjustments from time to time. As circumstances change and people mature and grow, relationships must adapt to stay in tune with these changes.

Often in marital therapy, couples are able to talk about the real issues in their relationship, finding that just stepping back from their busy life to gain perspective and discuss the state of their relationship is very beneficial and transformative. While counseling provides a supportive space for such reflections, it is even better for couples to set a regular time for family meetings. Additionally, we have to recom-mend to busy couples that they schedule special quality time with one another, away from the stresses of life.

For example, one couple, in the throes of what appeared to be an insurmountable impasse with the children, had never considered hiring a baby sitter and going out for a peaceful dinner, a temple function, or walk in the park. Upon being together without their rambunctious children, they remembered how much they had in common, and their natural love and appreciation for one another revived. They also decided that some parenting classes would give them tools for raising their children.

Offering sincere appreciation for our spouse can be a powerful elixir for our relationship, and thus we also often advise couples to offer sincere appreciation as a regular practice. Sounds simple, and yet it is very powerful.

Balance Builds Trust

Balance is also needed within the marriage relationship. There should be equal value between what each spouse gives to his or her partner and what each receives from the other partner. The specifics may differ in various settings, but there should be overall balance. For example, in traditional marriage roles, the husband may work hard providing an income and the wife may work hard caring for the children and other household affairs. If the individuals in the relationship feel the give-and-take is indeed balanced, each will feel that the relationship is fair. When this fair balance exists for a longer period, each will feel that their partner exhibits trustworthiness. This builds a sense of security that allows each to give freely to the other, without score keeping.

Trustworthiness is an essential element of relationships. Although love is a very important part of a marriage, trustworthiness has been found to have even more impact on the course of relationships,[5] as it is the foundation of love. Srila Prabhupada taught us that love and trust should be the basis of good devotee relationships and communities.

When there is an imbalance in the give-and-take, individuals may feel the deterioration of trustworthiness, and they may notice it manifest as anger, resentment, and the sense of being used. One example could be that a wife may work at an outside job and then come home to another 8 hours of household tasks while her partner chats online. The wife will likely become resentful; she may stop giving and may even take retaliatory actions.

If a partner receives respect and care, but does not give in return, that partner will likely feel some guilt, which may manifest as withdrawal or even as destructive forms of entitlement such as demands or threats.

It is important to remember that the balance of give-and-take does not need to be exact at every moment, but may oscillate appropriately between partners so that both partners give and receive in a way that balances over a period of time, and thus trustworthiness is established as result of this balance.

'Re-creation'

Part of creating balance and integration in your life is the concept of recreation.

> He who is regulated in his habits of eating, sleeping, **recreation** and work can mitigate all material pains by practicing the yoga system. [emphasis added]

> [*Bhagavad-gita* 6.17]

Recreation can also mean 're-creating' ourselves or gaining a fresh perspective on our life. Again, an apparently simple idea can revolutionize a stressed out, overworked couple; they can begin by scheduling quality time with one another. This time can remind both persons of goals they had forgotten, and they can plan ways to help facilitate each other's dreams for travel, occupation, or service.

One couple we worked with took a step back to get a big-picture view of their lives. As a result they were able to plan and carry out helping each other go back to school – one for an advanced degree, the other for a teaching certificate. The support they shared together strengthened their love, spirit of cooperation, and appreciation for each other, which also helped them feel more individually satisfied. They were able to offer more in charity to their local temple and to help start a Sunday school.

Krishna consciousness is serious, yet meant to be joyfully performed. Change of pace and variety can be very therapeutic, helping us feel renewed and refreshed. Looked at in this way, most devotees find it helpful for their spiritual life to have appropriate ways to do fun things as a family. Some devotees may work out or engage in sports to remain fit, while others may go to scenic places for a vacation. It is also essential to spend some fun time with your spouse to nurture your relationship. Ideally, our "fun" or recreation should be in the mode of goodness – favorable or supportive to our Krishna consciousness. Ultimately, we have to be the judge of this.

Varnashrama Dharma

> He who is regulated in his habits of eating, sleeping, recreation and **work** can mitigate all material pains by practicing the yoga system. [emphasis added]

> [*Bhagavad-gita* 6.17]

Varnashrama dharma is a timeless system for taking our emotional and physical realities into consideration while making spiritual advancement. This is echoed in the Buddhist expression of "right livelihood," which teaches that everyone has an ideal calling coupled with a higher divine purpose. Feeling satisfied in one's occupation is a significant part of being peaceful and fulfilled in life. Conversely, the lack of an occupational identity can cause distress and turmoil for a devotee. Real beauty is understanding one's material position and acting accordingly, without which one may be diverted from one's spiritual practice.

This perspective of balance and integration calls us to acknowledge our nature and dovetail[6] our desires. Srila Prabhupada said:

> [Arjuna] was a fighting man...After getting instruction of *Bhagavad-gita*....he said, "Yes, I shall fight." Now this is dovetailing. He, the fighting man, remained. The fighting man did not change into artist, or a musician. No. You need not change. You are fighting man; you remain a fighting man. If you are musician, you remain a musician. If you are a medical man, remain a medical man. Whatever you are, you remain, but dovetail it. Dovetail it.
>
> [Lecture on *Bhagavad-gita* 2.55-56 – New York, 19 April 1966]

> Even mundane activities dovetailed with service to the Lord are also calculated to be transcendental or approved kaivalya affairs.
>
> [*Srimad-Bhagavatam* 2.3.12, purport]

We started this chapter by quoting from *Srimad-Bhagavatam:*

> Steadiness in one's own position is declared to be actual piety, whereas deviation from one's position is considered impiety. In this way the two are definitely ascertained.
>
> [*Srimad-Bhagavatam* 11.21.2]

We have to know our actual level of spiritual advancement. This comes about from studying the scriptures with practical intent, consulting with advanced devotees, and, not least, being informed by our own practical experience. Feedback from our spouse can give us valuable insight; recurring complaints from our spouse are a very strong clue to follow up on.

As we mature, we will also come to understand our level of material necessity, which is the sum of the facilities, relationships, and objects that we need to get through this lifetime as a devotee fixed on the path of bhakti.

When we know our actual levels of spiritual advancement and material necessity, we can act accordingly by marrying, developing an appropriate occupation, or rarely, remaining a single renunciate living in a temple ashrama.

In my experience, "doing the needful" in progressive spiritual life will include the determination of our material necessity and our spiritual standing. The details of our lives will be different, but the goal of attaining Krishna consciousness is the same.

Dealing with Karmic Issues

> Even a man of knowledge acts according to his own nature, for every-
> one follows the nature he has acquired from the three modes. What
> can repression accomplish?
>
> [*Bhagavad-gita* 3.33]

With the increased self-awareness that spiritual life brings, we discover our past karma in the shape of conditioned habits and unresolved family-of-origin issues. These habits and issues impact our lives, causing relationship problems and imped-ing spiritual growth.

This is the stage of *Anartha nivrtti* I mentioned earlier, which involves becom-ing aware of habitual ways of thinking and acting, and then leaving them behind as unwanted baggage. These habits and issues need to be understood, dealt with appro-priately, and purified.

In addition to endeavoring to chant purely, being in saintly association, and engaging in introspection, many devotees have benefited from personal self-help processes, counseling, and psychotherapy. I spent many years sorting out my painful upbringing and childhood survival strategies that no longer served me, so I can also attest to the benefit of introspection, counseling, and focused spiritual practice.

We are meant to accept whatever is helpful for our progressive spiritual life. This is *yukta-vairagya*,[7] which means that one utilizes everything in the service of the Supreme Lord. Prabhupada also taught that "the proof of the pudding is in the tasting," which is to say that the value of anything is revealed by the results (*phalena pariciyate*).[8] Awareness of and lessening of our *anarthas*, coupled with spiritual advancement, are the results that speak of the success of our endeavors.

Focus on Spirituality in All Aspects of Our Life

The "Third Partner" in your Marriage – A useful tool in obtaining the proper balance in our life is to view Krishna as the "third partner" in our marriage. We can visualize a pyramid with husband and wife as the two bottom points, and the Lord at the top.

This concept helps keep our spiritual focus. Although basic physical, emotional, and spiritual compatibility is very important in marriage, our dedication to being Krishna conscious is the ultimate goal of our life and marriage.

Support Systems

It helps to have confidential friends and wise elders who can give us perspective on our life and marriage. Although we have to make our family decisions together with our spouse, in problem areas of conflict we can benefit from consultation with our "support system" of trusted friends, spiritual advisers, informed elders, and level-headed extended family members.

When counseling devotees, my wife and I often hear that they think their problems are unique. They are often surprised and comforted to hear that many of their issues are typical for couples and families. Groups of couples who meet regularly can also help each other know that they are not alone in their struggles. In this way devotees can become part of an extended family to create a culture of respect, compassion, and confidential practical support.

When is the last time you invited another couple or family over for dinner and planned a meaningful exchange? Please consider doing this soon!

You might find it helpful to record the results of your introspection using this chart:

'Balance Sheet'

Date:_____

Aspect or Area of My Life	Diagnosis			What Could Help? Next Steps	Support that I will ask from my spouse	Evaluation one month later
	In balance √	Needs balance √	Causing havoc! √			
Spiritual practices						
Marriage: quality time together						
Marriage: give and take						
Mental activity						
Eating						
Sleeping						
Keeping fit						
Recreation						
Work						
Effects of past karma						
Other:						
Other:						
Other:						
Other:						

Visit VaisnavaFamilyResources.org for a printable version of this chart.

Tips for Maintaining a Balanced Krishna Conscious Lifestyle

Some Common Challenges: Internal

- Thinking family duties are a hindrance rather than part of the process

- Thinking that family life means that spiritual life will automatically decrease

- Thinking that a family's spiritual program has to be identical to that at a temple (usually too long and complex to do at home); the "all or nothing" mentality

- Lack of enthusiasm especially regarding sadhana; feelings of hopelessness

Helpful attitudes:

- If I believe something is important, then I'll find a way to do it. Krishna will help

- It's not necessary to structure my family's spiritual program exactly like that of a temple; we can be creative

- Creativity and flexibility in general (home-based business, part-time work, ways of including the children in taking responsibility for part of worship, and so forth) can solve many seemingly insurmountable problems of integration

- Family life and spiritual life are not in opposition but support one another. Challenges, if met responsibly, help our spiritual growth

Some Common Challenges: External

- Work and/or school schedules which make regular spiritual practices at the same time each day difficult

- Not having good devotional means of recreation and therefore going for mundane sources of entertainment

Practical ways to integrate spiritual practices by having programs in the home:

- Having a scheduled time (which includes regulated sleeping)

- Set up a special place, such as an altar and temple room

- Encourage full family participation (not leaving the children sleeping; both husband and wife participating)

- Consider and discuss: should there be rewards/consequences for participation by the children?

- Join together with other families

- Eliminate disturbances (such as TV or activities that tend to keep people up late)

- If your family generally has a home program, consider a weekly scheduled temple visit

Practical ways to integrate spiritual practices by attending temple programs:

- Attend temples that have a program adapted to the needs of working families and school-attending children

- Establish a room for mothers with small children

- Establish a place in temples for toys and colouring for small children

- Cooperate with other families who want to establish family-friendly facilities

- If such facilities don't exist, try to constructively address such needs

The Power of Prayer

And finally, as we aspire for balance in the pursuit of the goal of loving and serving Krishna, we can take time to regularly pray for divine assistance in our life, our marriage, our family, and in the lives of others. Of course, there *are* a lot of things we can do to become balanced and Krishna conscious in our life and marriage, which I have outlined in this chapter. However, our ultimate success depends on the mercy of the Lord and His devotees. Although our endeavor and Krishna's mercy are both essential, we are absolutely dependent on His mercy. As Srila Prabhupada says:

> At such a time one can understand that Lord Sri Krishna's mercy is everything, that He is the cause of all causes and that this material manifestation is not independent from Him.
>
> [*Bhagavad-gita* 7.19, purport]

Our main spiritual practices of *japa* and *kirtana* are prayers to the Lord and His devotees. In addition we are advised by Srila Prabhupada in such writings as *Raja-vidya* and *Nectar of Devotion* to take all our confidential problems before the Lord, and to also pray for our perfectional stage.

Prayers by great saints and by our contemporaries inspire us; our own prayers address our personal issues. Through prayer, we empty out our heart and pray for help in our life as a devotee, spouse, parent, or friend.

Here are three of my more formal prayers:

I

> "My dear Lord, by Your will I have found a life partner, and I pray to always see my spouse as Your devotee – not as someone to use or dominate. Let us harmonize our differences in a balanced way, favorable to using our desires and nature in relationship to our spiritual practices. Let me assist my spouse in serving You, and also let me help all our family members have balance in their lives, with a focus on our path of bhakti."

II

"My dear Lord, please help me today fulfill the destiny You have planned for my life and marriage, by helping me make the appropriate choices for Your service, moment by moment. I know that in order to do this, I must live a life in harmony with Your instructions in scriptures and the advice of Your pure devotees, taking into account my particular nature and the necessities of my family. Let me keep my priorities in the proper place and my mind and heart focused on You. Please bless me to not be reactive to situations I find difficult, but to respond consistently with love, compassion, understanding, and wisdom."

III

"My dear Lord, please help me to attain balance in all areas of my life, by my taking proper care of my body, mind, emotions, intellect, and soul, in order to help foster attention to my spiritual practices. With this in place, let me serve the necessities of my family, my occupation, the society of devotees, the larger society of the world, and the universe. Examine my heart, and show me those places where I may be out of balance personally and in relationship to my spouse and family."

These prayers may help you develop your own; it is also good to just cry out with feeling.

Reflections and Questions on Balance

- If your life or marriage were in perfect balance – or even in better balance – what would it look like, and how would you feel differently than you do now?

- What areas of your life or marriage are out of balance, and what can you do to create balance? Consider the specific areas discussed in this chapter (and any more that come to mind), such as

  - your bodily health and activities to maintain it

  - mental attitudes

  - stress

  - occupation

  - creative outlets

  - natural ambitions and desires

  - family duties as a spouse

- family duties as a parent
- personal time and recreation
- your spiritual practices or sadhana

- Are you satisfied with your occupation? With your sadhana?

- What is the relationship between your spiritual practices and your occupational and family duties?

- If your life seems out of control, and you have tried your best both personally and with your spouse to come up with practical or creative solutions without success, is there anyone you respect that you can consult with? Would you consider counseling?

- Do you have a personal support system – a person or persons that you can share your problems and issues with? If not, would you consider looking for a devotee to be a confidential friend with? Would you consider finding a couple that could be confidential friends for you and your spouse? Would you consider finding or setting up a couple's group where you do spiritual practices together, as well as talk about pertinent issues?

Integrated Spirituality

Spirituality is the first and most important part of every devotee's life, yet it must be pursued in a realistic, uniquely individualized way, considering our material conditioning and necessities. The so-called material parts of life, such as earning a living, can be used to support our spiritual practice, and, in that sense, are actually Krishna conscious pursuits. We are advised by Srila Bhaktivinoda Thakur in his *Sharanagati*, or *Prayers of Surrender*, to accept what is favorable for our spiritual life, and to give up what is unfavorable – and this often changes at different times of our life.

In the grihastha ashrama, we must be spiritually-minded married persons, whose main aim is to progress spiritually. Being a balanced grihastha starts with understanding what is required physically, mentally, emotionally, and spiritually to be peaceful, happy, and fulfilled. By taking a long-term view of our goals, we can integrate all of those dimensions of our lives. With such balanced integrity, we can sustain the long haul – a lifetime (and beyond) of service to our guru, the devotees, and the Lord.

About the Author

KARNAMRITA DASA was initiated by Srila Prabhupada in 1970. For fourteen years, he lived in various ISKCON temples around the world. In the beginning of his devotional service, he participated in street *sankirtana* and book distribution, and eventually became a head cook and *pujari*, specializing in emergency devotional service. After marrying, he did extensive personal growth work and realized the importance of such healing as an adjunct to devotional service. Trained in many energy-healing modalities, he incorporates healing into his life, work, and service. He often works with his wife, Arcana Siddhi devi dasi, a licensed clinical social worker, in premarital counseling and couples therapy. Together they present workshops with spiritual and/or personal growth themes throughout the world. Karnamrita has a blog on Krishna.com and has recently released his first book, *Give to Live*, available through Amazon. He and his wife live and serve in Prabhupada Village, a small rural devotee community near Sandy Ridge, North Carolina, USA.

Chapter 10 Giving Back: Making a Social Contribution

Krsnanandini devi dasi

In this chapter you will learn:

✓ Why Grihasthas Should Give Back

✓ How Grihasthas Can Make a Difference in the World

✓ How to Deal with Challenges to Grihastha Giving

✓ The Grihastha Motto

Principles Highlighted in this Chapter

• Personal and Social Responsibility

• Regulated, Balanced, and Exemplary Lifestyle

Introduction

> This is a scientific movement for the good of the whole world. That you have to convince – by your character, by your behavior – then people will accept it.
>
> [Lecture on *Srimad-Bhagavatam* 1.10.03
> – Teheran, 13 March 1975]

A few years ago, my husband and I were on a flight returning from a SmartMarriages©
Conference. We had presented a workshop on Teaching Healthy Relationship Skills
to Couples. We both picked up an In-flight magazine and glanced at the lead article
when the words "Hare Krishna" jumped out at us. The author said that no one
would consider using the "Hare Krishnas" (devotees who chant "Hare Krishna")
as an example of anything. We took this as Krishna's mercy and a challenge for us
to work with others to reflect Srila Prabhupada's life-giving, empowering philosophy in the marriage and family arena. Right then and there, we envisioned flocks of
people coming to Hare Krishna communities requesting our advice and assistance to
create and maintain healthy, loving, principled families. In this chapter, you will find
ideas, suggestions, examples, scriptural references, and case studies that highlight the
social contributions that grihasthas, as spiritually practicing married persons, can and
should make in our Vaishnava communities and in the world at large.

Key Words for the Socially Responsible Householder

To illustrate the socially responsible householder, here are some key words to
consider:

Balance	Respect
Harmony	Loving service
Charity	Accountability
Example	Reliability
Dovetailing	Healthy recreation
Moderation	Cultural activity

Responsibilities of Krishna Conscious Marriage

Case Study of Serious Grihasthas – Kalindi dasi and Prema dasa (not their real names) signed up for relationship skill-building training before they had their fire sacrifice wedding ceremony. They wanted to get as much help as they could to prepare for a solid, healthy, and lasting marriage by developing effective communication and conflict resolution skills. Since they were both very serious about their devotional life, they wanted to understand the actual social and spiritual implications of grihastha life. Kalindi dasi and Prema dasa wanted to have realistic expectations about marriage and family life, and they understood that Srila Prabhupada recommended that couples get counseling before marriage.

Choosing to Live a Krishna Conscious Life – Making a choice to live a Krishna conscious life is the most important decision a person can make. When we find ourselves in the material world, it indicates that we have forgotten our perpetual divine connection as an eternal servant of the Supreme Personality of Godhead. Therefore, there is nothing more precious than reviving this everlasting relationship. Such a choice means a daily commitment to serving the Lord through instructions we receive from our guru, the shastras, and the sadhus, including saintly people past and present.

The Lord Himself has established the grihastha ashrama and the duties that are part of it. By His express will, there is a natural arrangement for progressive development through the ashramas. Inherent in each are requirements, that, when fulfilled, will propel the practitioners to the highest summit of self-realization. Devotees know this natural progression to be the varnashrama-dharma – a movement from brahmacharya (celibate student) to grihastha (married) to vanaprastha (retired), and finally – for some – to sannyasa (renounced monk).

Responsibilities of the Ashrama – When a devotee chooses the grihastha ashrama, the second rung of the spiritual ladder – one up from single or brahmachari life – he should understand that having a peaceful and healthy union includes accepting very serious social responsibilities. That is, married devotees are enjoined to care for elders, children, and those with infirmities; to give regularly in charity; to respect and care for Mother Earth; and to make wholesome contributions to the communities in which they live. Grihasthas are asked to be examples, encouraging others by their life, their words, and their actions. To this end, Srila Prabhupada states:

> We require so many householders to set the example for others, how in Krishna Consciousness we can live peacefully and sanely, even in married life. Also we require so many Krishna conscious children to show how nicely and beautifully a child can develop when he is following the principles of God consciousness.
>
> [Letter to Upendra, 9 December 1968]

Therefore, a Krishna Conscious Family is Socially Responsible

In the *Bhagavad-gita*, Arjuna asks the Lord, "What is the behavior of a devotee? How does he sit, walk, and talk?" Similarly, we can ask, what characteristics shine in a Krishna conscious family? How does the wife act? How does the husband behave? What are the expectations of the children?

A Krishna conscious family is socially responsible because husband, wife, and children not only cooperate to please Lord Krishna and to serve each other, but they treat other devotees and the people in general with love, appreciation, and respect.

> It is the duty of a householder to feed first of all the children, the old members of the family, the brahmanas and the invalids. Besides that, an ideal householder is required to call for any unknown hungry man to come and dine before he himself goes to take his meals. He is required to call for such a hungry man thrice on the road. The neglect of this prescribed duty of a householder, especially in the matter of the old men and children, is unpardonable.

> [*Srimad-Bhagavatam* 1.14.43]

We, my fellow grihasthas, have to make sure no one in our environment is hungry, especially older people and children! This is a powerful obligation. As we sincerely endeavor to comply with this grihastha duty, not only will we please the Lord, but we will become creative in our efforts to share Krishna Consciousness. This is an ideal example of how grihasthas should be selfless and socially concerned, and we have to consider *how to practically apply* this instruction in our own lives.

Now, depending on where we live, we may not run out into the street every time our family sits down for dinner. But we can prepare healthy nutritious *prasadam* and share with neighbors; we can make an effort to send or take cookies and other finger foods for school events when so requested; we can bring some *prasadam* to work with us to share with our co-workers. We can try to feed the *spiritual* hunger in our neighborhood by distributing books, brochures, and devotional music. Also, we can invite neighbors and co-workers or clients to the temple or a *nama hatta* program.

Two Basic Principles for the Socially Conscious Grihastha

Two of the Twelve Principles that are fundamental to healthy, progressive grihastha life are:

1. Personal and Social Responsibility

2. Regulated, Balanced, and Exemplary Lifestyle

These two principles highlight the duties that identify a God-conscious family. Listed below are some responsibilities that, when wholeheartedly embraced by husband, wife and children in a serious Krishna conscious family, fulfill the requirements for success in household life:

- They give in charity to worthy causes

- They support the other three ashramas – brahmachari, vanaprastha, and sannyasa

- They demonstrate how God-conscious families eat, work, worship, and play – teaching by the very way they live their lives

- They care for each other in loving, nurturing ways, practicing the six kinds of loving exchanges between devotees

- They are good neighbors

- They become expert in dovetailing all family and community activities for the pleasure of Krishna

Why Should Grihasthas Give Back?

So, why do conscientious grihasthas give back? Because we have been requested to do so by the Lord, and because we have faith that as we perform our duties, Lord Krishna will provide. In the words of an oft-cited Christian song,[1] "You can't beat God's giving, no matter how you try. The more you give, the more He gives to you. Just keep on giving, you'll find it's really true." By doing one or preferably all of the above actions, Krishna conscious family members effectively model the behavior of a healthy, loving, God-centered family. And there is a great need in human society to see the demonstration of strong, loving, God-conscious families who perform their duties well.

> One of the qualifications is *daksha*: he must be very expert in doing things very nicely. Not that because one is Vaishnava he'll be callous in the worldly things. No. Therefore I repeatedly request the management that you must be very expert in managing these temple affairs... Not a single farthing should be wasted. A Vaishnava must be *daksha*, expert in everything. This is no excuse, that 'I have become a devotee. Therefore I am callous to all material things.' What material things? *nirbandha-krishna sa-sambandhe yuktam vairagyam ucyate.* Anything in relationship with Krishna, that is not material; that is spiritual. I have several times explained that this temple, don't think it is ordinary building. It is Vaikuntha. *Cintamani-prakara-sadmasu.* Krishna has His house, *prakara-sadmasu. Cintamani-prakara-sadmasu. Sadma. Sadma* means house. So we should take very, very careful attention that this temple is kept very nicely, managed very nicely. Not that 'I have be-

come Vaishnava. Let everything be stolen or spoiled or broken. I have become Vaishnava. I cannot take care. That is not my consideration.'

[Lecture on *Srimad-Bhagavatam* 1.7.40
– Vrindavana, 1 October 1976]

Such a vision, seeing how to use everything in Krishna's service, was exemplified by Srila Bhaktivinoda Thakura, who composed the following prayer: "My house, my wife, my children, my wealth, they all belong to You O Lord."[2]

Engaging in these activities may often mean sacrifice. The Supreme Lord addresses this in the *Bhagavad-gita*, Chapter 18, Verse 5, "Acts of sacrifice, charity, and penance are not to be given up; they must be performed. Indeed, sacrifice, charity, and penance purify even the great souls." And in the purport to this verse, Srila Prabhupada explains,

> There are many purificatory processes for advancement of human society to spiritual life. The marriage ceremony, for example, is one of these sacrifices. The Lord says that any sacrifice which is meant for human welfare should never be given up. The marriage ceremony is meant to regulate the human mind to become peaceful for spiritual advancement.

[*Bhagavad-gita* 18:5, purport]

Artificial Renunciation: Another Illusion

To explore this topic, let's continue looking at our case study of Kalindi and Prema:

After spending more than 12 hours in premarital education sessions, Kalindi dasi and Prema dasa made plans to have their fire sacrifice marriage ceremony with the help of family and friends. At the wedding, they listened intently as the brahmana minister spoke. He explained that sincere devotees who get married should understand that the grihastha ashrama or spiritual family life is one of the four ashramas, a place of spiritual growth as opposed to *griha-medhi* life, which is marriage based on sense gratification and material enjoyment without God at the center. Within the grihastha ashrama, the priest explained, devotees take their family responsibilities seriously, and they shouldn't artificially or prematurely relinquish their marriage duties. The Lord Himself emphasized this when He appeared on the earth about 500 years ago as Lord Chaitanya:

> Lord Chaitanya said to a devotee, "Be patient and return home. Don't be a crazy fellow. By and by, you will be able to cross the ocean of material existence. You should not be a show bottle devotee and become a false renunciate. For the time being, enjoy the world in a befitting way but do not get attached to it. Within your heart, you should keep

yourself very faithful but externally, you may act like an ordinary person. Thus Lord Krishna will soon be pleased with you and deliver you from the clutches of maya."

[*Chaitanya-charitamrita, Adi* 15.26-27]

Challenges: I Understand My Duties as a Grihastha, But...

As a grihastha, you have realized that you are accountable for caring for children, elders and others less fortunate. Like Kalindi dasi and Prema dasa, the couple from our case study, you also accept the responsibility of supporting the other three ashramas, and in your heart you really want to give the recommended percentage of your income to promote Krishna consciousness – yet, there are still some challenges to your fulfilling these duties. Some possible obstacles to fulfilling your social responsibilities might be as follows:

- Feeling that you don't have adequate income to maintain your family

- Being sometimes confused about what is material activity and what is spiritual activity in your family life

- Being unsure about how to come up with creative non-financial ways to support or serve

- Not being part of a spiritual community, thus often feeling that you and your family are struggling alone

Vaishnava Social Responsibility in Action – To get some idea of how to resolve these challenges, let's explore some past and present examples of Vaishnava social responsibility in action:

- Lord Chaitanya staying in Puri, Orissa, upon the request of his mother – an example of caring for needs and concerns of a mother

- Srila Bhaktisiddhanta bringing a jacket for Srila Prabhupada's son at Radha Kunda – an example of a guru caring about the needs of his disciples

- Srila Prabhupada telling Brahmananda dasa to pay obeisances to his mother – showing how we should respect our parents and elders

- Srila Prabhupada walking across the yard to turn off a neighbor's dripping water tap – demonstrating a bold act for conserving natural resources

- Srila Prabhupada telling a devotee to serve his jail term, saying that Krishna would protect – showing how devotees should respect the laws and tolerate consequences of their own negative actions

- Srila Prabhupada talking to an older neighbor lady in Philadelphia regarding her health and grandchildren – showing how we should be neighborly and friendly to devotee and non-devotee alike

- Srila Prabhupada giving money to Chitralehka devi dasi for her children – exemplifying that we should diligently take care of the physical as well as spiritual needs of our children, and that good leaders care about all of the needs of their followers

- Srila Prabhupada not parking in restricted parking in Alachua, Florida, at midnight – teaching us that devotees should be exemplary citizens

- Ambarisa dasa and Lekhasravanti dasi donating money to purchase the Fisher Mansion, now the Detroit temple – showing devotees endeavoring to give 50% (or more) of their income in the service of the Lord

- His Holiness Bhakti Tirtha Swami setting up a health fund for Vaishnavas – Krishna conscious leaders showing compassion and affection for their followers and others through setting up systems or institutions that perpetuate their care

- Many, many devotees who prepare *prasadam* for distribution in places such as schools and homeless shelters – showing how devotees work to alleviate both material and spiritual hunger in their communities

- Temples who use earth-friendly, ecologically-sound disposable plates, cups, and spoons in their *prasadam* distribution – illustrating the Vaishnava commitment to caring for Mother Earth and living carefully on her

- Devotees who take special care not to waste *prasadam* and who encourage others in the same way – demonstrating appreciation for the mercy of the Lord and the principle of utility

- The many thoughtful and generous devotees who share Krishna's loving message with those who are incarcerated, writing to them and sending them literature through prison ministries

- Grihasthas cooperating with other families to fulfill their duties, such as sharing child-care, and caring for each other when illness or challenges arise

As grihasthas, we have a unique opportunity to teach by the way we live and to create, join, or support spiritual communities. Carrying out our daily duties, including our morning program and service to the Deity, caring for our families in loving ways, supporting the other ashramas, giving regularly in charity, and being an asset in our communities, grihasthas can reflect practical, God-centered family life, and attract others to do the same.

The 50% Dilemma

The concept of giving 50% of one's income to the service of the Lord is exemplified by Srila Rupa Goswami, the leader of the Gaudiya Vaishnavas, and suggested by Srila Prabhupada as a goal to which all householders could aspire. This Krishna conscious principle is more than a little intimidating to many devotees. Frequently, given their financial situation, devotees cannot even imagine how they could live on half of what they currently earn. The application of this principle has bewildered or intrigued devotees everywhere. What exactly does this mean? Does this mean 50% of gross income? Or of net income? Or after bills have been paid?

In *Nectar of Instruction*,[3] we learn that being attached to following rules and regulations without understanding the purpose or goal of these rules and regulations can spoil one's devotional service. So, instead of worrying about how the percentage should be calculated, let's try to grasp the purpose and expediency of this charitable principle:

- Everything belongs to Krishna, therefore, when we offer something in the service of the Lord, it's just acknowledging the rightful owner or returning the property to its rightful owner.

- Giving is a way to show love – giving gifts, *prasadam*, money, time, and talents. Spiritual life is a culture of giving.

- Giving charity is a sacrifice that purifies one's wealth. If wealth is not purified, it will often be taken through unexpected expenses such as fines, legal fees, medical bills, taxes, or theft.

- Even a little, given in the service of God, rewards the giver hundreds and thousands of times.

- Srila Prabhupada said that this movement is creating people who are "independently thoughtful." He wanted us to use our intelligence and creativity in carrying out scriptural instructions in cooperation with other devotees.

The idea here is to begin some way to ***consistently*** give a certain percentage in charity, to support the mission of Krishna consciousness. Start by giving a manageable amount, maybe 10% of your net income, to a cause, initiative, or program that is implementing the mission of the Supreme Lord. Plan to gradually increase this percentage. For householders, this is a blessed and necessary duty. In addition to supporting your local temple or *nama hatta* program, there are so many projects to choose from – those that promote causes such as Krishna conscious education, healthy community life, book distribution, and Vaishnava care. When the Lord sees your steady commitment to giving in charity, He will give you intelligence and facility to do so – from within and without.

Krishna will give you intelligence how to engage in honest, brilliant, glorious work on His behalf. There is no need to engage in anything dishonest. Krishna has given enough money, now earn by honest means.

[Letter to Alex, Bob, Drdhavrata, Gupta, Rsabhadeva and Stan, 24 January 1977]

More Examples of Social Contributions for Grihasthas

Some other significant social contributions for grihasthas include the following:

- **Being conscious of our effect on Mother Earth** and the environment, living as ecologically awarely as possible – using items that can be re-used and recycled, being thrifty, not wasteful.

- **Living a simple, uncluttered life but thinking highly.** Many people in the western culture are collectors, using storage facilities and overloading their houses with things that require attention to clean, to store, to pack, or to move. Eliminate things that cannot be utilized in Krishna's service, avoid greed, take care not to collect too much.

- **Giving in charity** – aim to give a consistent percentage of your income to Krishna conscious causes, support the mission, support devotee care – children, elders and brahmanas.

- **Regularly distributing books and prasadam** in both traditional and creative ways.

- **Having regular family meetings** to share and discuss family activities, goals, and services.

- **Being good, caring, conscientious neighbors and relatives.**

- **Taking very good care of your family responsibilities** – doing so with love and dedication. Study the example of Srila Prabhupada, who ensured that his family would be provided for although he took sannyasa.

- **Doing fun activities with your children and your spouse.** Real spiritual family life is not boring drudgery. Play, healthy personal connection, and cultural activities that uplift through music, drama, and art should be an accepted part of grihastha life.

"R" You Ready for the Grihastha Motto?

Therefore, a good motto for the socially conscious grihastha is contained in the "Seven R's" which are **"Reclaim, Recycle, Reduce, Restore, Recreate, Reflect, and Recite."** Let's take a look at some of the ways that one couple, Mira and Nala, show social responsibility through implementing the Seven R's.

1. **Reclaim** our spiritual birthright by engaging in devotional service.

   Mira and Nala, in their seriousness about reconnecting with the Lord, have both taken initiation into Krishna consciousness and committed to observing the four basic principles (no illicit sex, no gambling, no intoxication, and no meat-eating). They plan to save money this year so that Nala can attend a 24-hour kirtan and Mira can attend the annual Vaishnavi retreat.

2. **Recycle** by re-using things in Krishna's service.

   Mira is determined to recycle; in their household, she and the rest of the family diligently collect plastic, paper, and other recyclables and make sure these items go in the recycle bin. When clothing or other household items are no longer usable, she makes a special effort to give to others or to agencies that distribute them. Mira also persuaded her temple authorities to use recyclable plates and utensils for programs.

3. **Reduce** waste, clutter, and *anarthas* (unwanted things both spiritual and material)

   In an effort to reduce waste, Nala and Mira adhere to a budget. One way they encourage their children not to waste is by giving them smaller servings of *prasadam*. The children can always ask for more if they like. For a long time, Nala was challenged by his past hoarding habits. He collected books, papers, tools – always something he planned to use or give to others. While reading Rupa Goswami's *Nectar of Instruction*, he saw that collecting too much is a cause of a spiritual fall-down. He decided, much to Mira's relief, to de-clutter the garage and some of the living areas in their house.

4. **Restore** wholesome family and community life through service, charity, and personal example.

   Mira and Nala, motivated by a desire to make a contribution to their neighborhood, went door to door to meet their neighbors, offer them *prasadam*, and invite them to a monthly yoga program in their home. When they sat down to look at their budget, Mira and Nala made a commitment to give a total of 15% of their income, calculated after setting aside savings and paying their monthly bills. They chose to help support two initiatives: Srila Prabhupada's book distribution program and the Grihastha Vision Team's efforts to strengthen Krishna conscious families.

5. **Recreate** by finding positive recreation – family games and cultural activities to share with family and friends.

    Weekly family meetings are very important in the Mira-Nala household. No phone calls, computer, or television are allowed to disrupt these regular family sessions. Sometimes they play games with their children or watch an inspirational or devotional movie. They use these weekly meetings to check in with one another, talk about and assign chores, or establish and review family/couple goals. They are also a part of a monthly Grihastha Support Group of couples who visit each other's homes for *sadhu-sanga, prasada,* and fun educational couple activities.

    _____

6. **Reflect** daily on the words of the Lord and His devotees.

    Even though they have two young children and have less free time because of work and the care of the children, Mira and Nala made a pact to read at least 15-30 minutes every day from one of Srila Prabhupada's books. They also endeavor to read Krishna stories to the children just before bedtime.

    _____

7. **Recite** the holy names of the Lord.

    After practicing Krishna consciousness for over three years, Mira and Nala conscientiously endeavor to keep their vow to chant at least 16 rounds of the Hare Krishna mantra every day. They have a small altar in their home and try to chant devotional songs at least once a day.

    _____

> Please take the time now to write down at least one action that you and your family can do in each of the seven categories of the Grihastha Motto.
>
> If you like, you can write your action on the line under Mira and Nala's action in the examples of the "Seven R's" above.

The World Cries Out For Grihastha Examples of Responsibility and Care

In today's world, as in the past, most people will get married, and they need to see examples of healthy, socially conscious householders who are beacons of light. Srila Prabhupada gave direction for all of his disciples when he told us that "Utility is the Principle, Preaching is the Essence, Books are the Basis, and Purity is the Force." Husband and wife can evaluate the utility of their activities to determine if these activities can be offered to the Lord; they can share Krishna consciousness in creative ways; they can read and distribute books; and they can affect their environments by their sincere, pure endeavors.

In the end, a sincere householder realizes that married life is a status of great responsibility. In fact, human life, as distinguished from lower animal life, means responsibility. As grihasthas who fulfill our responsibilities in a mood of loving surrender to the instructions of guru and Krishna, we will be instruments of peace and hope, and make steady progress on the path of spiritual perfection. Then, folks from many different backgrounds will want to know how the Vaishnavas have such supportive, caring, spiritually-enlivened marriages and families. So much so that one day, a devotee flying on an airplane will pick up an in-flight magazine and read an article about how married people would do well to follow the examples of the "Hare Krishnas."

About the Author

KRSNANANDINI DEVI DASI is a minister, a Certified Family Life Educator (CFLE), President of the Grihastha Vision Team, Co-Director of the Dasi-Ziyad Family Institute (www.dzfi.org), and dedicated mother of ten children. Raised in a Christian family, Krsnanandini studied Islam, Mormonism and other religions to appreciate the underlying unity in all the world's religions. On Radhastami, September 12, 1972, she was initiated into Vaishnavism by Srila Prabhupada in Dallas, Texas, and has been a practitioner of bhakti-yoga, the yoga of love and devotion, since that time.

Along with her husband, Tariq Saleem Ziyad, she has served hundreds of individuals and couples, providing them with healthy relationship skills. She and Tariq have designed and/or implemented several workshops and curricula relating to marriage, family and youth, including the Young Pioneer Project, the S.E.L.F. Healthy Relationship Course, From Couple to Couple Mentor Couple Training, *Parenting for the 21st Century*, a 16 lesson curriculum for a variety of parents – and more. Krsnanandini devi dasi appeared in the documentary "SpiritWorks" and in "ONE: The Movie" with Deepak Chopra, Ram Dass, Thich Nhat Hanh, and Bhakti Tirtha Swami. She is author of the "Booklet of 8's: A Concise Guide to Spiritual Living", *How to Raise Your Children Spiritually,* the *First Book of Hare Krishna Puzzles, Quizzes and Riddles,* and contributor to the book *All-In-One Marriage Prep: 75 Experts Share Tips & Wisdom to Help You Get Ready Now.* She and her husband travel around the globe spreading the message that with a serious spiritual foundation, people can learn skills and make commitments to create and maintain healthy, happy relationships and marriages.

Concluding Words

Partha dasa

JUST PRIOR TO SITTING DOWN to write these concluding words, my attention was caught by research done in the United Kingdom on the reasons couples divorce. The major reason cited was "growing apart."

> **Growing apart now trumps extramarital affairs as the No. 1 cause of divorce in the U.K., according to a survey of divorce lawyers. Since accountancy firm Grant Thornton started publishing its annual matrimonial survey in 2003, infidelity had been the biggest marriage killer.**[1]

The word **growing** attracted my attention since I have a large vegetable garden and several flower beds. Keeping them in a healthy state requires at least 3 hours a week doing simple activities like weeding and watering. Occasionally a bear needs to be chased away before it eats a row of carrots or every single apple on my tree. If I neglect this basic maintenance, the vegetables and flowers become stifled by a vast variety of weeds.

Most summers, I leave my garden for two weeks to attend Janmastami and Ratha Yatra in Vancouver. On returning, I am welcomed by the most astounding display of insidious flora. How, in two weeks, this sinister vegetation could get bigger than the tender veggies I had been cultivating for two months is a mystery of the universe! Getting things back to normal is not just a matter of making up the missed 6 hours – it takes me at least 12 hours.

Marriage relationships are bit like that. For a husband and wife to "grow together," it requires regular nurturing. Ignore that nurturing, and weeds can sprout and choke out the sense of connection. Unfortunately, the "happily ever after" fairy tale paradigm of marriage may cause couples to expect marriage to be an effortless, endless romance. Tragically, when such neglect causes couples to "grow apart," they may exist in parallel disjointed worlds or even consider ending their relationship.

We can be negligent, becoming distant, our heart and soul connection hidden by weeds, or we can grow together nurturing that connection. The choice is ours. Feeling love is not an entitlement, rather it is the fruit of cultivating loving acts.

There are many weeds that can stifle heart to heart connection: poor communication, stonewalling, misunderstandings, misconceptions, selfishness, callousness, resentment, stubbornness, being unfaithful, being negligent, being disrespectful, failing at compassion, failing to appreciate, failing to care, failing to serve, failing to listen, failing to be affectionate, failing to be considerate, failing at empathy, failing to connect, failing to collaborate, failing to trust, failing to be trustworthy, failing to remember, false expectations, faulty paradigms...the list could go on and on.

On the other hand, growing together requires a much shorter list: mutual love, compassion, and service. And chasing out any of the above-mentioned bearish behaviors that sneak in!

Out of caring and deep concern, the GVT has produced this book to offer you, the reader, a vision and tools to nurture a healthy heart and soul connection. We, the authors, would like to end by extending to you the sincere intent behind our chapters.

Chapter 1: Foundations: Twelve Principles for Successful Krishna Conscious Family Life

I pray that all followers of Srila Prabhupada will learn to honor and relish the Twelve Principles for Successful Krishna Conscious Family Life. These principles and values are important tools that guide us in creating joyful spiritual family life. Taking these principles to heart promotes purity, faith, a service attitude, and genuine love and care for our worldwide devotee family.

Your servant,
Praharana devi dasi

Chapter 2: Ready or Not, Here I Come: Preparation for Marriage

I pray that the information in this book will help you to ascertain your real needs, so you can connect with a like-minded soul who will inspire you to live your values.

Your servant Uttama devi dasi

Chapter 3: Let's Talk About it: Open and Honest Communication

May you be blessed with the desire and ability to deeply communicate, through words, body, and action, with your spouse and family. Communication works for those who work at it, and it is most certainly worth the effort.

Your servant,
Mantrini devi dasi

Chapter 4: Roles of the Husband and Wife in the Vaishnava Community

I pray that these few examples will inspire you, the reader, to always look at how you can apply the revealed principles to your own life in a way that will benefit all in your sacred space, especially Lord Krishna.

Yours in peace and unity,
Tariq Saleem Ziyad

Chapter 5: Krishna's Economics: Spiritualizing Your Wealth

I pray that all of the readers can learn to use Krishna's resources in a way that will be compatible with their spiritual journey. And that those who are grihasthas can live a harmonious prosperous life together with Krishna in the center.

Your servant Arcana Siddhi devi dasi

Chapter 6: Affection and Physical Intimacy: The "Hot Potato"

I pray that our discussion on this subject will assist you in navigating this sensitive topic with mutual openness, honesty, understanding, and compassion, today and through the evolution of your marriage.

Your servant Partha dasa

Chapter 7: Sacred Parenting: What Krishna Conscious Parents Want to Know

My prayer for you, dear reader, is that this chapter sensitizes you to take parenting to a new level with the understanding and knowledge you have gained from it. My prayer is that you feel a deep connection with your children, your own self, your spouse, and Krishna, and that you become a highly effective parent.

Your humbly grateful servant,
Sridevi dasi

Chapter 8: Marriage Under Attack: Dealing with Serious Conflict, Separation, and Divorce

Dear reader: Our prayer is that you may be able to do the little things that make a big difference in your relationships. May you have the strength of heart to utilize the tools and principles presented in this chapter and throughout the book to continue to grow and be inspired in all of your relationships.

Your servant Krsnanandini devi dasi

Chapter 9: A Balanced and Sustainable Marriage

My prayer for you is that you may catch the essence of balance and find it helpful in your life as a devotee, spouse, and parent. Achieving integration in our spiritual life is the central point; it is the sun around which every facet of balance revolves. I also pray to Srila Prabhupada and Sri Chaitanya that you may consider the members of the GVT your friends in service, providing you with useful tools and ideas to help you have a great marriage which fosters your spiritual progress.

Your servant Karnamrita dasa

Chapter 10: Giving Back: Making a Social Contribution

"Sarve sukhino bhavante" – "Let everyone be happy." We pray that you become empowered to be good examples of loving, peaceful, socially responsible families and supporters of Lord Krishna's mission in this world.

Your servant Krsnanandini devi dasi

We, the Grihastha Vision Team, pray that you will choose to take up these tools and produce the fruits of strong, healthy, loving Vaishnava marriages. These fruits will benefit not just you and your spouse but also your children, your grandchildren, your community, and your society, and be pleasing to Srila Prabhupada and Lord Krishna.

The End

Discussion Guide: Suggested Questions for Individual or Group Study

These study questions can be used for creating a grihastha group for mutual support of marriages. They are only possibilities; the group can create other questions based on the needs of the group.

Grihastha groups, meeting monthly, can be a tremendous support and inspiration using the Vaishnava loving exchanges of hearing in confidence and sharing insights. They can help one realize that one's experiences are 'normal,' that most couples experience similar stages in their marriages. Other group members may offer helpful insights and support to transition through difficult times. Such meetings can also provide meaningful social interaction that can be enhanced by the inclusion of kirtan and prasadam.

Chapter 1: Foundations: Twelve Principles for Successful Krishna Conscious Family Life

1. Why is it important to clarify and understand the principles and values you want in your family?

2. What two principles do you implement most in your family?

3. What two principles do you struggle with most in your marriage?

4. Without looking at the book, see if you can recall at least 8 of the 12 Principles for Successful Krishna Conscious Family Life.

Chapter 2: Ready or Not, Here I Come: Preparation for Marriage

1. Discuss what your specific expectations for marriage are (or, if you are married, what your specific expectations were).

2. What skills do you think are the most important ones to bring to a relationship? Why?

3. What strategies have you found useful for dealing with differences?

4. If you thought you married the wrong person, but treated them like the 'right' person, what do you think could happen?

Chapter 3: Let's Talk About It: Open and Honest Communication

1. Discuss the difference between an "I" message and a "You" message. Why do "I" messages work better? Practice using "I" messages with each other about current disagreements.

2. What is the "Speaker-Listener" technique? How does it lead to empathic listening? How can you use this technique in your marriage? Take turns being the speaker and listener as you discuss an important issue in your marriage.

3. What is the difference between our "intent" in communication and our actual "impact"? Discuss ways to find out what our impact is on the other person and how to make our intent more clear.

4. What are some of the filters that distort communication? Make a list of some good ways to deal with filters in your communication with your spouse.

Chapter 4: Roles of the Husband and Wife in the Vaishnava Community

1. Why can't every couple have the same specific roles and/or duties for the husband and the wife?

2. What are some of the factors that determine which roles you play in your family?

3. How can the examples of great Vaishnava couples from the past help us in determining the role of a husband or a wife in a Krishna conscious marriage?

4. How can we utilize the principle of Spiritual Equality / Material Difference to assist us in figuring out what roles we accept in our marriage?

5. "Without having Mutual Respect and Appreciation, a couple cannot properly function in their roles." Explain why this is true or false.

Chapter 5: Krishna's Economics: Spiritualizing Your Wealth

1. Are you a 'spender' or a 'saver'? How does this impact your life and relationships?

2. What are your biggest fears about money? If you can, share the stories about what caused them and how you are trying to overcome them.

3. Are your money arguments about money or about what money means to you? Discuss the possible emotional needs behind 'money' arguments.

4. Discuss the benefits of applying the principle of Krishna's Economics; also discuss why it can be difficult.

Chapter 6: Affection and Physical Intimacy: The "Hot Potato"

1. How has the modern portrayal of love and intimacy in the media affected you and those around you?

2. Why is it hard to express your needs?

3. Brainstorm some good connection rituals. Find a time to discuss developing your personal connection ritual with your spouse.

Chapter 7: Sacred Parenting: What Krishna Conscious Parents Want to Know

1. Look back at the parenting style chart. What parenting style were your parents using while they raised you? What aspects of their parenting led you to identify that style? How has this impacted your views on parenting? How has this impacted your actual parenting in stressful situations?

2. What parenting style were your spouse's parents using while they raised your spouse? How has this impacted your spouse's parenting?

3. Discuss the parenting style chart with your spouse. Share with your spouse how the parenting style of your parents has impacted your parenting, or has caused differences of opinion between the two of you.

4. Share one of your parenting challenges with the group, along with what you found that worked or didn't.

5. Try Reflective Listening with a young person. Share your experience with the group.

Chapter 8: Marriage under Attack: Dealing with Serious Conflict, Separation, and Divorce

1. What grade would you give your marriage? A, B, C, or D? ("A" being spiritually and materially satisfying, a real teamship, a good example for others, and "D" being frustrating and de-energizing) Compare notes with your spouse.

2. Look over the warning signs listed in this chapter. If you detect one or more of these signs, discuss ways to improve your relationship in those areas, and seek advice from the group. What suggestions from this chapter might be helpful for a troubled marriage? Identify at least one thing that you can do to improve your relationship with your spouse.

3. Are you willing to get help if your marriage needs it? Why or why not?

4. Write down the positive qualities that attracted you to your spouse in the beginning of your relationship. Share this with your spouse, and think of things you can do together that will improve your relationship.

5. Identify your default style for dealing with conflicts. Remember, identifying your default style is the first step for choosing more effective solutions.

6. Take one area of conflict, and argue from your spouse's perspective.

Chapter 9: A Balanced and Sustainable Marriage

1. Write down areas of your life that seem out of balance; think about how they could cause conflicts in your marriage. Share your answers with your spouse, and ask for feedback and possible solutions.

2. Talk about the areas of your life that are out of balance (or could be more harmonious) with the group and see how others have dealt with similar problems.

3. If your sadhana (spiritual practices such as japa, kirtan, and reading scripture) has been neglected due to the pressures and responsibilities of marriage and family life, ask your spouse how the two of you, together, can make sadhana more of a priority.

4. Is there is an activity you and your spouse (and/or family) could do together that would provide you opportunities for "re-creation"? Is there a possible time to step back from your life to reflect and gain clarity in a peaceful location such as a park or the ocean? Would doing this regularly help you become more balanced in your life and family?

Chapter 10: Giving Back: Making a Social Contribution

1. If you aren't regularly tithing or giving a percentage of your income to a spiritually worthy cause you believe in, how can you begin to do it?

2. Why is tithing and giving in charity important for grihastha couples? What are the benefits? Are there any disadvantages?

3. Explore possible projects that a group of grihasthas in your area might do together which would benefit the local temple or association of devotees in your area. For example, you could cook the Sunday feast together, serve prasadam, put on a play or workshop, or help a devotee family in need.

4. Talk about some things you and your family could do (e.g. starting a nama hatta group by having regular spiritual gatherings at your home, participating in some type of outreach such as sankirtan, group chanting in the street, book distribution, and college programs) to acknowledge the gift of Krishna consciousness that you have received.

5. What are some ways you and your family engage (or could engage) in the Seven R's of a Krishna Conscious Family – The Grihastha Motto: "Reclaim, Recycle, Reduce, Restore, Recreate, Reflect, and Recite"?

Resource Guide: Suggested Reading

T HE FOLLOWING BOOKS are ones that members of the GVT have found useful regarding marriage and family. As with any non-devotional literature, some 'swanning' may be needed – in other words, being like the swan by taking the essence and disregarding any undesirable values. Naturally, our favorites are largely compatible with Krishna conscious values.

Communication:

How to Talk So Kids Will Listen & Listen So Kids Will Talk by Adele Faber and Elaine Mazlish (New York: Avon Books, Inc. 1999)

Nonviolent Communication: A Language of Compassion by Marshall B Rosenberg (Encinitas, California, PuddleDancer Press, 2000)

The Five Love Languages: How to Express Heartfelt Commitment to Your Mate by Gary Chapman (Northfield Publishing, 1992) ISBN: 1881273156

Marriage Preparation:

How to Avoid Falling in Love with a Jerk: The Foolproof Way to Follow Your Heart without Losing Your Mind by John Van Epp (McGraw-Hill, 2008)

All-in-One Marriage Prep: 75 Experts Share Tips & Wisdom to Help You Get Ready Now by Susanne M Alexander (Naples, Florida: Barringer Publishing, 2010)

Marriage Enrichment:

How to Improve Your Marriage Without Talking About It by Patricia Love and Steven Stosny (New York: Broadway Books, 2008) ISBN: 0767923170

CompassionPower.com

Dasi-Ziyad Family Institute: www.dzfi.org

Vaishnava Family Resources: www.VaisnavaFamilyResources.org

The Seven Principles for Making Marriage Work: A Practical Guide from the Country's

Foremost Relationship Expert by John M Gottman and Nan Silver (New York: Three Rivers Press, 1999) ISBN: 0609805797

The Science of Trust: Emotional Attunement for Couples by John M Gottman (W. W. Norton & Company, 2011)

The Relationship Cure: A 5 Step Guide to Strengthening Your Marriage, Family, and Friendships by John M Gottman (New York: Three Rivers Press, 2002), ISBN: 0609809539

The 7 Habits of Highly Effective Marriage by Stephen R Covey (FranklinCovey, 2008)

The Five Love Languages: How to Express Heartfelt Commitment to Your Mate by Gary Chapman (Northfield Publishing, 1992) ISBN: 1881273156

World Class Marriage: How to Create the Relationship You Always Wanted with the Partner You Already Have by Patty Howell (Rowman & Littlefield Publishers, 2010) ISBN: 1442203250

Divorce Busting: A Step-by-Step Approach to Making Your Marriage Loving Again by Michele Weiner-Davis (New York: A Fireside Book, 1993) ISBN: 0671797255

Parenting:

How to Talk So Kids Will Listen & Listen So Kids Will Talk by Adele Faber and Elaine Mazlish (New York: Avon Books, Inc. 1999)

Kids Are Worth It!: Giving Your Child The Gift Of Inner Discipline by Barbara Coloroso (New York: HarperCollins, 2002)

Parenting for the 21st Century, a 16 lesson comprehensive, interactive curriculum by Krsnanandini Dasi & Tariq S Ziyad to teach empowering parenting skills to today's parents. Order and information at www.dzfi.org

Nonviolent Communication: A Language of Compassion by Marshall B Rosenberg (Encinitas, California; PuddleDancer Press, 2000)

Screamfree Parenting: The Revolutionary Approach to Raising Your Kids by Keeping Your Cool by Hal Edward Runkel (New York: Broadway Books, 2008)

Setting Limits with Your Strong-Willed Child: Eliminating Conflict by Establishing Clear, Firm, and Respectful Boundaries by Robert J MacKenzie (New York: Three Rivers Press, 2001)

1-2-3 Magic: Effective Discipline for Children 2-12 by Thomas W Phelan (Glen Ellyn, Illinois: ParentMagic, Inc. 2010) ISBN: 0963386190

Surviving Your Adolescents: How to Manage – and Let Go of – Your 13-18 Year Olds by Thomas W Phelan (Glen Ellyn, Illinois: ParentMagic, Inc. 2010) ISBN: 1889140082

Homeschooling Krishna's Children by Aruddha Dasi (Second Avenue Books, 2012)
KrishnaHomeschool.org

Affairs:

The Monogamy Myth: A Personal Handbook for Recovering from Affairs, Third Edition
by Peggy Vaughan (New York: Newmarket Press, 2003) ISBN: 1557045429

*Not "Just Friends:" Protect Your Relationship from Infidelity and Heal the Trauma of
Betrayal* by Shirley Glass (New York: The Free Press, 2003) ISBN: 074322549X

My Husband's Affair Became the Best Thing That Ever Happened to Me by Anne Bercht
(Vancouver: Trafford Publishing, 1997) ISBN: 1412033209

Abuse:

*Love Without Hurt: Turn Your Resentful, Angry, or Emotionally Abusive Relationship
into a Compassionate, Loving One* by Steven Stosny (Da Capo Press, 2008)

Money

Financial Peace Revisited by Dave Ramsey (Viking Penguin, 2003)

Get a Financial Life: Personal Finance In Your Twenties and Thirties by Beth Kobliner
(A Fireside Book, 2009)

Debt-Free Forever by Gail Vaz-Oxlade, host of the TV show 'Till Debt Do Us Part'
GailVazOxlade.com/resources/guide_to_building_budget.html

*The 9 Steps to Financial Freedom: Practical and Spiritual Steps So You Can Stop
Worrying* by Suze Orman (New York: Three Rivers Press, 2008)

The Road to Wealth by Suze Orman (Riverhead Press, 2010)

Notes

Foreword

1. Srila Rupa Goswami's *Bhakti-rasamrta-sindhu* is a Sanskrit work composed in the early 16th century. The title translates as 'Nectar of Devotion,' which is likewise the title Srila Prabhupada gave to his summary study of this important book.

2. Frank Pittman, *Grow Up! How Taking Responsibility Can Make You a Happy Adult* (St. Martin's Press, 1998)

Chapter 1

1. *Bhagavad-gita* 8.15

Chapter 2

1. "Marriage with a view to peaceful and virtuous life and with a view to procreate servants of the Lord is a good institution for a Vaishnava." Nine principal doctrines quoted in chapter 22 of *Seventh Goswami* by Rupa Vilasa dasa

2. *Srimad-Bhagavatam* 3.21.16

3. Steven Stosney, *Love without Hurt: Turn Your Resentful, Angry, or Emotionally Abusive Relationship into a Compassionate, Loving One* (Da Capo Press, 2008) CompassionPower.com

4. John Van Epp, *How to Avoid Falling in Love with a Jerk: The Foolproof Way to Follow Your Heart without Losing Your Mind* (McGraw Hill, 2007)

5. ibid

6. Steven Stosney, *Love without Hurt: Turn Your Resentful, Angry, or Emotionally Abusive Relationship into a Compassionate, Loving One* (Da Capo Press, 2008) CompassionPower.com

Chapter 3

1. Nancy J Wasson, co-author of *Keep Your Marriage: What to Do When Your Spouse Says "I don't love you anymore!"* KeepYourMarriage.com

2. John M Gottman, *The Seven Principles for Making Marriage Work: A Practical Guide* (New York: Three Rivers Press, 1999)

3. Gerard Egan, *The Skilled Helper: A Problem-Management and Opportunity-Development Approach to Helping*, Ninth Edition (Brooks/Cole, Cengage Learning 2010)

4. Howard Markman and Scott Stanley, PREP©: The Prevention and Relationship Enhancement Program www.PrepInc.com

5. ibid

6. This statement from the *Adi Purana* is quoted by Srila Prabhupada in *Nectar of Devotion* Chapter 12: Rendering Service to Devotees

Chapter 4

1. John Gray, *Men are from Mars, Women are from Venus: A Practical Guide for Improving Communication and Getting What You Want in Your Relationships* (HarperCollins, 1992)

2. Alvin Toffler, *Future Shock* (Random House, 1970)

3. *Bhagavad-gita* 7.8, purport: "One who knows God knows that the impersonal conception and personal conception are simultaneously present in everything and that there is no contradiction. Therefore Lord Caitanya established His sublime doctrine: *acintya bheda*-and-*abheda-tattva* – simultaneous oneness and difference."

Chapter 5

1. The Apostle Paul in a letter to Timothy: 1 Timothy 6:10 (King James Version)

2. "According to Vedic principles, a householder, before taking lunch, should go outside and shout very loudly to see if there is anyone without food. In this way he invites people to take prasadam. If someone comes, the householder offers him prasadam, and if there is not much left, he should offer his own portion to the guest. If no one responds to his call, the householder can accept his own lunch. Thus the householder's life is also a kind of austerity. Because of this, the householder's life is called the grihastha-ashrama." (*Chaitanya-charitamrita, Madhya* 3.41) See also *Srimad-Bhagavatam* 1.14.43

3. Lecture on *Srimad-Bhagavatam* 3.25.38 – Bombay, 7 December 1974

4. Syamasundara dasa recounts the story of the hundred dollar bills in the *Memories* book, Vol. 2, p.327

5. *Srimad-Bhagavatam* 7.11.25, purport: "Canakya Pandita gives a very valuable instruction: *dampatyoh kalaho nasti tatra srih svayam agatah*. When there are no fights between husband and wife, the goddess of fortune automatically comes to the home."

Chapter 6

1. *Srimad-Bhagavatam* 1.1.22: "… the difficult ocean of Kali, which deteriorates all the good qualities of a human being." Srila Prabhupada comments in the purport that "In this age, the life span will gradually decrease. People will gradually lose their memory, finer sentiments, strength, and better qualities.")

2. David Frawley, *Ayurvedic Healing: A Comprehensive Guide* pg. 192 (Twin Lakes, Wisconsin: Lotus Press, 2000)

3. In classical Sanskrit, a Sloka is the most commonly occurring four line verse of poetry.

4. *Bhagavad-gita* 2.64: "...a person free from all attachment and aversion and able to control his senses through regulative principles of freedom can obtain the complete mercy of the Lord."

Chapter 7

1. Krsnanandini Devi Dasi and Tariq Saleem Ziyad, *Parenting for the 21st Century* (Cleveland Heights: Dasi-Ziyad Family Institute, 2006)

2. Diana Baumrind, "Child-care practices anteceding three patterns of preschool behavior" *Genetic Psychology Monographs* (1967)

3. Barbara Coloroso, *Kids are Worth It: Giving Your Child the Gift of Inner Discipline*, revised edition (HarperCollins, 2010)

4. EE Maccoby and JA Martin, "Socialization in the context of the family: Parent–child interaction." In P Mussen and EM Hetherington, editors, *Handbook of Child Psychology, volume IV: Socialization, personality, and social development*, chapter 1, pages 1–101. Fourth edition (New York: Wiley, 1983)

5. Based on the study of parenting patterns by Diana Baumrind

6. Family Wellness Associates, founded by George Doub and Virginia Morgan Scott, based in Salida, California

7. *Srimad-Bhagavatam* 5.5.18: "One who cannot deliver his dependents from the path of repeated birth and death should never become a spiritual master, a father, a husband, a mother or a worshipable demigod."

8. *Srimad-Bhagavatam* 10.45.3, purport: *kaumaram pancamabdantam / paugandam dasamavadhi / kaisoram a-pancadasad / yauvanam tu tatah param* "The *kaumara* stage lasts until the age of five, *pauganda* up to age ten and *kaisora* to age fifteen. From then on, one is known as *yauvana*."

9. Jean Piaget's observation of children led him to postulate four stages of cognitive development: sensorimotor stage (birth to age 2), preoperational stage (age 2 to 7), concrete-operational stage (ages 7 to 12), and formal-operational stage (ages 12 and up)

10. Erik Erikson's observation of human development led him to postulate eight life stages of psychosocial development

11. Barbara Coloroso, *Kids are Worth It: Giving Your Child the Gift of Inner Discipline*, revised edition (HarperCollins, 2010)

12. Aruddha Dasi, *Homeschooling Krishna's Children* (Second Avenue Books, 2012) KrishnaHomeschool.org

Chapter 8

1. Visakha devi dasi, "Serving Krsna as a Husband or a Wife: What Makes It Rough, What Makes It Smooth" ISKCON Communications Journal, Volume 9 Number 1, September 2001 content.iskcon.org/icj/9_1/visakha.html

2. *Srimad-Bhagavatam* 8.22.29-30

3. John M Gottman, *The Seven Principles for Making Marriage Work: A Practical Guide* (New York: Three Rivers Press, 1999)

4. From Chaitanya Mahaprabhu's "Shikshastaka Prayers" found in *Chaitanya-charitamrita, Antya* 20.21

5. Roger Fisher and William L Ury with Bruce Patton, editor, *Getting to Yes: Negotiating Agreement without Giving In* (Penguin Books, 1991). Behavioral scientists Kenneth Thomas and Ralph Kilmann, who developed the Thomas-Kilmann Conflict Mode Instrument (1970), have identified five styles to responding to conflict – competition, collaboration, compromise, avoidance, and accommodation. No conflict style is inherently right or wrong, but one or more styles could be inappropriate for a given situation and the impact could result in a situation quickly spiraling out of control.

Chapter 9

1. Stephen R Covey, A Roger Merrill, and Rebecca R Merrill, *First Things First: To Live, to Love, to Learn, to Leave a Legacy* (Simon & Schuster, 1994)

2. ibid

3. Srila Rupa Goswami, *Bhakti-rasamrta-sindhu* 1.4.15-16

4. "If one offers Me with love and devotion a leaf, a flower, fruit or water, I will accept it. Whatever you do, whatever you eat, whatever you offer or give away, and whatever austerities you perform – do that, O son of Kunti, as an offering to Me." (*Bhagavad-gita* 9.26-27)

5. Terry D Hargrave and Franz Pfitzer, *Restoration Therapy: Understanding and Guiding Healing in Marriage and Family Therapy* (New York: Taylor and Francis Group, 2011)

6. 'Dovetail' is a carpentry reference to a type of joint used to connect two pieces of wood together, using shapes that are flared like a dove's tail. A dovetail joint is very strong, effectively making the two pieces of wood stand as one integrated unit.

7. Srila Rupa Goswami, *Bhakti-rasāmṛta-sindhu* 1.2.255-256: "When one is not attached to anything, but at the same time accepts everything in relation to Krishna, one is rightly situated above possessiveness. On the other hand, one who rejects everything without knowledge of its relationship to Krishna is not as complete in his renunciation." Quoted in *Bhagavad-gita* 6.10, purport.

8. *Srimad-Bhagavatam* 8.9.28

Chapter 10

1. "You Can't Beat God Giving" was composed by brilliant African American gospel writer and singer, Doris Akers (1923-1995)

2. Srila Bhaktivinoda Thakura's song "Manasa Deha Geha" can be found in *Songs of the Vaisnava Acaryas*

3. Srila Rupa Goswami, *Nectar of Instruction* 2

Concluding Words

1. Toronto Sun www.torontosun.com/2011/08/31/affairs-no-longer-leading-cause-of-divorce-survey reviewing the 2011 Grant Thornton matrimonial survey: www.grant-thornton.co.uk/PageFiles/3537/Matrimonial_Survey_2011.pdf

Glossary of Terms

diksha: spiritual initiation. The *diksha-guru* is the spiritual master who connects one with the Supreme Lord through initiation. A disciple has only one *diksha-guru* but may also have any number of *shiksha-gurus* (instructing spiritual masters). See also 'shiksha'.

grha-vrata or **grha-medhi:** one who is attached to the material duties of family life.

gurukula: literally, 'the guru's family;' a teacher's ashrama where traditional education is given.

japa: the soft recitation of the holy names as a private meditation, with the aid of 108 prayer beads.

nama hatta: literally, 'the marketplace of the holy name;' a place other than a temple where devotees gather to hear and chant about Krishna.

prasadam: literally, 'mercy;' food prepared for the pleasure of Krishna and offered to Him with love and devotion. Because Krishna tastes the offering, the food becomes spiritualized and purifies anyone who eats it. When sattvic foods (milk, grains, fruits, vegetables, sugar, and legumes) prepared by a devotee are offered to the Deity of Krishna as prescribed in the system of bhakti-yoga, the offering is transformed into *prasadam*, the mercy of the Lord. Food offered to Krishna is free of karma. By accepting Krishna's *prasadam*, one can rapidly become purified and achieve pure love of God.

pujari: a devotee who performs the direct worship (puja) and service for the Deity in a temple.

sadhu-sanga: the association of saintly persons.

samskara: Vedic purificatory rites of passage.

sankirtan: congregational chanting of the names and glories of Krishna, which is the most recommended method for spiritual success in the current Age of Kali.

shiksha: spiritual instruction. See also 'diksha.'

Vaikuntha: the Spiritual World; literally, 'the place free from anxiety.' The kingdom of God, full of all opulences and unlimited by time and space.

yukta-vairagya: real renunciation by utilizing everything in the service of God.

Who's Who: Historical Persons

A. C. Bhaktivedanta Swami Srila Prabhupada (1896-1977): Founder-*Acharya* of ISKCON and foremost presenter of Krishna consciousness in the Western world. For more biographical information see *Your Ever Well-Wisher* and *Srila Prabhupada-Lilamrta* as well as the movie serial *Abhay Charan*.

Advaita Acharya (1434-1539): A notable disciple and companion of Chaitanya Mahaprabhu; the guru of Haridasa Thakura. For his history, see *Chaitanya-charitamrita*.

Arjuna: The third of the five Pandava brothers, he lived approximately 5,000 years ago. He figured prominently in winning the Kurukshetra war, with Krishna driving his chariot. It was to Arjuna that Krishna spoke the *Bhagavad-gita* just before the battle. See the *Mahabharata* for more information.

Bhakti Tirtha Maharaja (1950-2005): A sannyasi disciple of Srila Prabhupada, later a guru in ISKCON; an African-American seeker who rose from impoverished conditions in the Cleveland ghetto to become a global spiritual leader. For more of his life story, see *Black Lotus: The Spiritual Journey of an Urban Mystic*, Stephen J Rosen (Hari Nama Press, 2007)

Chaitanya Mahaprabhu (1486-1534): Krishna Himself in the role of His own devotee. He taught the pure worship of Radha and Krishna, primarily by sankirtana, the congregational chanting of Their names. He is also remembered in the history of Bengal as a great social reformer who pioneered civil disobedience and worked against the caste system. For more information, see *Chaitanya-charitamrita* and Prabhupada's Introduction to *Srimad-Bhagavatam*.

Devahuti: The daughter of Svayambhuva Manu; wife of the sage Kardama; mother of the Supreme Lord's incarnation Kapila. Lord Kapila taught Devahuti the science of pure devotional service through a study of the elements of creation. For more of her history, see the Third Canto of *Srimad-Bhagavatam*.

Draupadi: The wife of all five Pandavas, she lived approximately 5,000 years ago. Both she and her twin brother, Dhrishtadyumna, were born to help destroy the Kuru dynasty. An attempt to disrobe her in a royal assembly doomed the Kurus to annihilation. She figures prominently in the *Mahabharata*.

Haridasa Thakura (1451-1530): Raised Muslim, he became a friend and disciple of Advaita Acharya and a great devotee of Lord Chaitanya Mahaprabhu. He is known as the *namacharya*, the master who taught the chanting of the holy names by his own example. For more of his history, see *Chaitanya-charitamrita*.

His Divine Grace A. C. Bhaktivedanta Swami Srila Prabhupada (see A. C. Bhaktivedanta Swami Srila Prabhupada)

His Holiness Bhakti Tirtha Maharaja: (see Bhakti Tirtha Maharaja)

Kunti: The mother of the Pandavas, she lived approximately 5,000 years ago. For more of her history, read the *Mahabharata*, *Srimad-Bhagavatam*, and *Teachings of Queen Kunti*.

Lord Chaitanya: (see Chaitanya Mahaprabhu)

Narada Muni: A great devotee of Lord Krishna who travels throughout the spiritual and material worlds singing the Lord's glories and pointing the way to the path of devotional service. He tells his own life-story in the First Canto of *Srimad-Bhagavatam*.

Prahlada Maharaja: As the five-year-old son of the mighty demon King Hiranyakashipu, Prahlada disobeyed his father by worshiping the Personality of Godhead and telling his classmates about His glories. Hiranyakashipu tried every possible way to kill the young prince, but failed to harm him. Finally Lord Nrisimha killed Hiranyakashipu and enthroned Prahlada as king of the demons. Prahlada's history is found in the Seventh Canto of *Srimad-Bhagavatam*.

Radharani: Krishna's original pleasure potency, from whom all His internal energies expand. She is His eternal consort in Vrindavana, the leader of the *gopis*, and the most dedicated and beloved of His devotees.

Srila Bhaktisiddhanta Sarasvati Thakura (1874-1937): The spiritual master of A. C. Bhaktivedanta Swami Prabhupada; a scholar and scientist who discovered Pluto; the son of Srila Bhaktivinoda Thakura. He campaigned strongly against the caste system in spite of threats against his life. He was the first to present Gaudiya Vaishnava philosophy to the Western world. *A Ray of Vishnu* by Rupa Vilasa dasa is a biography of Srila Bhaktisiddhanta Sarasvati Thakura.

Srila Bhaktivinoda Thakura (1838-1914): An acharya in the Gaudiya Vaishnava disciplic succession; a magistrate in the British Raj; in charge of the Jagannatha temple in Puri; prolific poet and song-writer who wrote '*Jaya Radha-Madhava*,' the *Gaura arati* song, and the prayer before honoring *prasadam* ('*sarira avidya jal*') among many others; and the father and grand spiritual master of Bhaktisiddhanta Sarasvati Thakura. *Seventh Goswami* by Rupa Vilasa dasa is a biography of Srila Bhaktivinoda Thakura.

Srila Prabhupada: (see A. C. Bhaktivedanta Swami Srila Prabhupada)

Srila Rupa Goswami (1489-1564): The leader of the Six Goswamis of Vrindavana, who were the principal followers of Chaitanya Mahaprabhu. Srila Rupa is the prime authority on the science of *rasa*, loving exchanges with God, which he explained in his *Bhakti-rasamrita-sindhu* and *Ujjvala-nilamani*. He was also an eminent playwright, poet, and archeologist, identifying and preserving the lost holy places in Vrindavana. Most Gaudiya Vaishnavas consider themselves *rupanugas*, followers of Rupa Goswami.

Srila Vishvanatha Chakravarti Thakura (1626-1708): A prominent Gaudiya Vaishnava *acharya* in the line of Srila Narottama dasa Thakura. In the mid seventeenth century he lived at Radha Kunda and wrote commentaries on *Srimad-Bhagavatam*, the *Bhagavad-gita*, and the works of the Six Goswamis. Srila Prabhupada dedicated *Bhagavad-gita As It Is* to Srila Vishvanatha Chakravarti Thakura.

69396811R00131

Made in the USA
Columbia, SC
15 August 2019